W9-DHU-409

Justice At The City Gate

Justice At The City Gate

Social Policy, Social Services, and the Law

Susan G. Neisuler

Writers Advantage

New York Lincoln Shanghai

Justice At The City Gate
Social Policy, Social Services, and the Law

Writers Advantage
an imprint of iUniverse, Inc.

For information address:
iUniverse
2021 Pine Lake Road, Suite 100
Lincoln, NE 68512
www.iuniverse.com

All client names are fictitious, with the exception of Denise Gallison, whose case was widely covered. Department of Social Worker names, with the exception of those who created especially praiseworthy policies, are fictitious.

ISBN: 0-595-26950-8

To my favorite guys:

Ross F. Neisuler, my husband
Peter G. Neisuler and Justin A. Neisuler, my sons

ACKNOWLEDGMENT

I could not have written this book without the continuing support of my editor, Rose Glickman, who couched her criticisms of my verbose writing style in gentle words of encouragement.

My hat is off to all librarians everywhere, in particular, those at the Newton Public Library and the Massachusetts State House Library. They helped to make my research a pleasure rather than a chore.

And, thank you—all you social workers, supervisors and directors in Massachusetts and across the country who took the time out of overcrowded days to spend time talking with me.

Last, but by no means least, I want to acknowledge the enthusiastic, unwavering support my husband, Ross Neisuler, gave to this project. He never doubted, though at times I did, that this book could and should be written. With the deepest gratitude I want to say, "Thanks, Ross."

CONTENTS

INTRODUCTION

Children and their families are at the heart of social welfare programs. These programs are as old as the first English settlements in the New World and as recent as the Administration of William Jefferson Clinton. The goals of social welfare programs for the poor derive from the goals the larger society has for itself. In turn, economic development, political organization, social stability, and family integrity influence decisions about who is needy and how to help them. Social welfare programs require a redistribution of resources, from the "haves" to the "have-nots." Americans have always been reluctant to redistribute wealth, holding instead to their faith in *laissez-faire* and individualism. The country values the private economy over the public, and values individual autonomy over collective choice.

The American welfare state was not born until the Great Depression, when President Franklin D. Roosevelt allowed the federal government to be the political and financial vehicle that moved Americans from unemployment to employment. The welfare state was intended to have a short life. As Roosevelt explained in his 1935 State of the Union address, "The continued dependence upon relief induces a moral and spiritual disintegration. The federal government must and shall quit the business of relief." He said this at a time when the program had taken a very thin slice off the unemployment statistics. The future for aid did not look promising when the nation's premier engineer of aid programs referred to them in such condemnatory terms, even in the dark days of depression.

Because social welfare goals touch the deepest core of American ideology, they tend to polarize Americans. Funding programs for children and the elderly vie with programs for work training. Conflicts also develop over the nature of the welfare offered. Should help be offered in cash or in kind? Rent supplements or public housing? Should a family receive help in order to keep its children at home, or should the public moneys be spent on institutions and foster homes to house the children? Should cash payments be tied to work-incentive programs, or given with no strings attached? What, in fact, is the nature of human nature? Does it respond to punishment? to incentives? or to some combination of the two?

A policy that resolves these conflicts can be formulated only when the underlying need and common social values come together. For example, twentieth-century Aid to Dependent Children followed the path first put in place by the nineteenth-century policy of funding widows' pensions. That is, the breadwinner, by definition a worthy person, had died, leaving his wife and children destitute. In such circumstances the government could adopt a policy that it should give assistance to the family. This acceptance of the individual's needs coincided with society's consensus that the healthy development of children required that they remain in their own home with their mother and siblings rather than relocate to an institution or go off to live with strangers. The public was willing to spend public money to support this policy.

Conversely, the Center for Disease Control in Atlanta, Georgia, may have evidence to suggest that the nation's health would improve if there was nationwide distribution of clean, free hypodermic needles. However, since there is no common support for free, clean hypodermic needles, no public policy can develop in either case.

The formulation of social welfare policy is a political process. In America, there is no special god to pay homage to, or king to mollify. Policy is made by powerful interests that use money to influence political decision-makers, by organized citizens who use their voting strength, and by the occasional leader who envisions a policy that would serve the country, and who secures support for it.

After all is said and done, Americans do not approve of welfare programs. The nation is captive to the historical myth that *everyone* has a fair chance to move up the ladder. This leaves only a narrowly-defined group of the truly infirm that they see as deserving of help. Americans are fondest of that part of their history in which the thirteen colonies rose up to slay the Goliath King George because he levied taxes arbitrarily. Such icons of memory have left us with welfare programs that are fragmented, disparate, and under-funded.

Social welfare policy provides the framework within which child welfare policy, theories about the nature of the family and children, juvenile and family law, and social service agency policy developed. This book looks at three hundred years of these policies, and the way they intersect one another.

CHAPTER ONE

SOCIAL SERVICES,
TODAY AND YESTERDAY

CHAPTER ONE

Social Services, Today and Yesterday

"Let justice reign at the city gate."

Amos, Old Testament Prophet

Introduction

"I have no choice," the judge said, "but to order Liza Barrow and her sister into the custody of the Department of Social Services." As one of the attorneys representing the family, I was appalled. The judge was making a mistake. The girls needed their mother more than ever. Couldn't the judge see the obvious—a mother, father, children, and grandmother clinging to each other, devastated by Liza's experience of sexual abuse. But Judge Johnson, responding to the petition of the Department of Social Services, was holding the parents responsible for the sexual abuse of their daughter.

The family, through its attorney, pleaded, "Your honor, we think we know who did this, and when." The Barrow parents proceeded to describe an afternoon when the extended family, including distant relatives, gathered to mourn their newborn infant's recent death. At some point family members realized that Liza and a particularly unsavory uncle had disappeared. Then came the discharges on her panties and a trip to the hospital emergency room. Now, although they had a credible story about the identity of the perpetrator, Judge Johnson cast a suspicious eye on the father, Carl Barrow. She ordered that this traumatized little girl and her sister be removed from the home of their mother and father.

Mr. Barrow offered to move out of the house until the investigation was completed.

"My mother lives just a few blocks away," he explained, "I can live with her until you think it's safe to let me back."

The attorney for the Department of Social Services, the agency that summoned the family to court, said,

"No. We will not allow that."

The maternal grandmother, present in the courtroom, also lived in the area. She urged the court, "Let me take the girls, Judge. At least they can be with family." The department attorney said that he would have to check to make sure no one in the family had a criminal record.

When Attorney Donnell returned, he reported that the criminal records check revealed that years ago a son who had lived in the grandmother's house was found to have molested one of his sisters. Department policy forbade placing a child in such a home.

Both the grandmother and the mother of the child at the center of the immediate hearing exclaimed, "Judge, that was a foster son. He left the house, and none of us has seen him for years!" The grandmother added, "If he came back, I would never let him stay."

The girls were crying.

Judge Johnson was disconcerted. "But," she said, "I have no choice." The Supreme Judicial Court of Massachusetts has ruled that a Department's decision can only be overruled if a judge finds that it has "abused its discretion" (i.e., done something outrageously wrong). Judge Johnson felt that this case did not qualify. The Department's decision stood and the girls were placed in foster care.

In sum, the Department of Social Services, charged by the legislature and the citizenry at large with protecting the Commonwealth's children, adhered to a policy that, in this case, intensified the emotional distress of a young child.

In 1919, when Massachusetts established its first child-protection agency, its newly appointed director said the public could measure its success by asking five questions: Has it protected and made happier the unfortunate and neglected children of the Commonwealth? Have individuals, officials, and other societies turned to it with a better understanding of its purposes and its power to render service? Has its staff become more sensitive to the abuses of children, and at the same time become more intelligent in the use of all the social, medical, and legal remedies that our communities provide? Has it contributed to a better understanding of the conditions that continue to wreck or maim children's lives? Has it learned to dovetail its work with that of other agencies so as to reduce duplication and increase effectiveness?

The answer to these questions became a resounding NO after an egregious case of child death and brutality caused the agency to close its doors and reorganize in 1974. The newly structured Department of Social Services reopened its doors in 1980. Observers familiar with the current Massachusetts Department of Social Services would issue the same judgement when answering those original five questions: Unequivocally, NO.

To understand how we reached such a point, we need to understand the origins of American attitudes toward children, families, and people in need of services. We have to start with the Puritans.

Who were the Puritans?

"God Almighty in His most holy and wise providence hath so disposed of the condition of mankind, as in all times some must be rich, some poor, some high and eminent in power and dignity; others mean and in subjection."

John Winthrop, the first Governor of the Massachusetts Bay Colony, "A MODEL OF CHRISTIAN CHARITY," Boston, 1630

The men and women who arrived on the coast of Massachusetts between the years of 1620 and 1630 were profoundly English. In particular, they were a special kind of English: angry, rebellious, religious, fierce, and independent English. They were quick to judge, quick to punish. Their very lives were at risk, with no safety net to catch them. The Plymouth colony had an additional, practical reason to fear poverty: the colonists were joint stockholders in the enterprise that funded their voyage. Their fellow investors expected to be repaid. These circumstances and their particular personalities led them to work harder than it is possible for a twentieth-century American to imagine. They were braver and more steadfast than it is possible for a twentieth-century American to imagine. They carried their faith with them so completely that no thought, no behavior, no law, or policy could exist independently from it. They believed that nothing was more revered than the individual conscience, that one owed one's chief allegiance to God and to the community.

Where did that faith come from? It began as a break from the Protestant Reformation, a reformation within the Reformation. Like the original Reformation, its goal was to cleanse a church that had departed too far from the original, simple teachings of Christ; its claim was that the Church of England was in need of purification. The spiritual, moving force behind this formulation of religious doctrine was John Calvin, a theologian from Geneva.

Calvinism was a very demanding faith. It urged unrelenting hard work. This hard work would result in visible success, which would prove that God was indeed looking with favor on the particular person. That person would then be one of the Elect. Being a deserving Elect was very close to being holy. Conversely, to be poor or idle (one and the same) was to have brought Satan to the community. This was a bitter threat to the righteous. John Winthrop, the first Governor of the Massachusetts Bay Colony, personally opposed a pay raise to carpenters and artisans of three shillings a day, lest it enable them to work four days instead of five and spend the remainder of their week in "vain and idle time." And in 1672, the colonial legislature made it illegal for an adult to lure a child away from his work or studies because they believed the child would become idle (evil) as a result.

The belief that hard work and prosperity were proof of God's favor framed the thinking of the founders as the colony of Massachusetts responded to "the poor and needy." Of course, there were many poor and needy, especially in the very first decades of colonial life. Winter was especially dreaded. For the first ten years of the Plymouth Colony, every winter brought a "starving time." The need for public assistance could not be ignored. The first English law of public assistance, with which the colonists were deeply familiar, and which they followed for the next three centuries, had as its basis the celebrated Elizabethan Act of 1601 For the Relief of the Poor.

Poor Laws, or Puritan social welfare policy

By the late sixteenth century, the British government had perceived that punitive measures directed at its vast and growing number of vagrants were insufficient to preserve civic order because, as a social historian once observed, "the whip had no terror for the man who must either tramp or starve." Based on the idea that poverty was an economic rather than a personal matter, and that the state should help those people who could not provide for themselves, a series of measures relating to poverty, vagrancy, and relief of the poor had been enacted. These measures attempted to deal with the problem of economic insecurity in light of changing religious, social, and economic conditions of the period. The series of laws that culminated in the Elizabethan Poor Law of 1601, the mother of all Poor Laws, established the principle of *relief locally financed and administered for local residents*. It distinguished three major categories of dependents—the vagrant, the involuntary unemployed, and the helpless. Vagrants who refused to work could be committed to a house of correction, whipped, branded, put in pillories and stoned, or even put to death. Parents were legally liable for the support of their children and grandchildren. Children for whom parents could not provide were to be bound out as apprentices.

The long-term background of the famous statute was a century's worth of social and economic dislocation. By 1600, the growth of cities, increasing industrialization, and large-scale agricultural production made people more economically interdependent. The collapse of feudalism removed the safety net that generations of peasants had relied on, for better or for worse. It cast large numbers of people with no means of earning a living adrift on the land. The immediate background was the worsening times of the preceding decade, a decade of food scarcity and widespread famine, of insecurity and great suffering. Rioting, thievery, and social disorder became widespread. Lawmakers, fearful of insurrection, felt compelled to order and organize the administration of charity and the enforcement of work. The 1601 Elizabethan Poor Law stood, with only minor revisions, for almost 250 years.

The essential feature of the Elizabethan Poor Law was that the local church parish administered it. Two corollaries, the Principal of Settlement and

Removal and the Principal of Primary Family Responsibility, supported the Poor Law.

"Settlement and removal" meant that only those people recognized as bona fide settlers in the parish had the right to request aid. Charity stopped at the borders. If a stranger made the request, no aid would be given. The request would most likely be met by the demand that the person (or family) be removed from the parish.

In New England, the distribution of charity lay in the hands of New England Calvinists. Whatever instinct for charity there may have been was muted by the spiritual need of the community to maintain among them, at the minimum, a token number of poor. This seeming anomaly existed because helping out the poor and "people of an inferior sort" gave the wealthy an outlet for carrying out their God-ordained task. The poor could remind their better-off neighbors how much closer to God they were. The poor were necessary, but their "idleness" could not go unpunished. In 1633, the Massachusetts General Court provided for harsh treatment for those who spent their time "idly" or "unprofitably;" they were bound as indentured servants, whipped, run out of town, or jailed.

Measures were necessary to meet the needs of the community in a more immediate sense: orphaned boys were apprenticed to craftsmen or farmers; orphaned girls were assigned to families to do housework, childcare, etc. in return for free room and board. The economic and religious unit of "one man, one woman" was considered so basic to survival that the widows and widowers who were still alive after a harsh winter were sometimes re-distributed and married to each other.

Other ways of handling the destitute were tried. Seventeenth-century communities typically sought out a family that would accept some (very small) payment, generated by the town, to board a fellow citizen who was without shelter. The town of Hadley, Massachusetts, for example, voted at its town meeting in 1687 to send a certain widow "round the town" to live with each family able to receive her (in this case, however, there is no record of money being offered).

All this sounds as though, even in the midst of privation, the colonists were able to maintain a sense of the need for succor and aid to the poorest..

However, this was not the case if the most needy were unknown to the community (i.e., the "strangers" referred to previously). Ancient concepts of feudal ties to a native place and parish seem to have worked their way into the colonists' minds, already overloaded with concerns about resources. The "stranger" was going to cost the townspeople money they felt no requirement to pay. A stranger could be an itinerant, an artisan who went from town to town looking for work, or a seaman just pulled into port.

Regardless of the reason, the laws regarding strangers were straightforward and severe. As early as 1636, Boston's selectmen prohibited citizens from entertaining strangers for more than two weeks without securing official permission. Those who came without permission were "warned away." This warning out became a "due process" tool: unless persons were warned to depart from the town within three months of their arrival, they could gain settlement there, *and the town would be liable for their support if they became dependent.*

Expulsions could result in extreme hardship. Death from exposure or Indian attacks was not uncommon. Family ties did not change the harsh verdict of the town fathers. The Chelmsford, Massachusetts, town records reveals one such event: In January 1670, notice was given to Henery Merrifield that he had to "discharge" his daughter, Funnell. In December 1671, Merrifield's wife was summoned before the Selectmen to answer for entertaining their Funnell "contrary to towne order." When she answered that Funnell was their daughter and she could not turn her "out of doars this winter time," the Selectmen only replied that they would suspend a penalty until the County Court sat and heard the case.

Immigration and Almshouses

Immigration to the colonies exploded in the eighteenth century. The population grew from 350,000 in 1710, to 1.5 million in 1760, to 2.5 million in 1775 (Note: The population of England and Wales was 6.7 million at the time). Twenty-two percent of this population was black, 90% of whom lived as slaves in colonies south of Pennsylvania. Most of the white immigrants were from the British Isles. They were fleeing the powerful effects of England's primogeniture laws, which disinherited the sons who were not first born thus causing them to flee to the cities where they joined the unskilled urban masses. People were also fleeing the effects of England's rapid industrialization: overcrowding, disease-ridden cities, extreme poverty and want, and a rigid class system. And, finally, they were fleeing the religious conflicts that embroiled all Englishmen regardless of class.

The tendency, broadly speaking, was for the strongly committed English Calvinists to go to New England, as all colonies in New England were founded and led by religious leaders. The less religious English, along with other nationalities (German, Dutch, Swedes, French Hugenots), migrated to the middle colonies of New York, Pennsylvania, and Delaware. Catholics, and those fleeing the Puritan reign of Oliver Cromwell (1649 to 1660), migrated to the South—Maryland for Catholics, and South Carolina for the upper classes that had lost the war against Cromwell. Of course, on any ship headed for the colonies, there was a random collection of the talented, the criminal, the energetic, and the desperate—in short, the composite American immigrant.

Having a large immigrant population meant having a large number of "strangers" in your midst. "Strangers," as we have seen, were in a different category from settlers. Although there was no legal or religious obligation to come to the assistance of needy strangers, the vast increase in population made such measures as "warning out" impossible.

Almshouses

By 1700, the need to take care of the poor in the cities had grown so great that Boston appointed four full-time "overseers of the poor." An overseer in poor law legislation could be the person who determined who was poor, who provided the relief, or who directed the operations of an almshouse. Sometimes, but not always, the position included a stipend.

Town fathers did not look further than the almshouse for a "solution" to the problem of the needy. Boston had erected its first in 1660. In 1692, the colonial legislature, in a very limited attempt to appoint someone to be responsible for the poor, passed a law specifying that family members were primarily liable for the support of needy relatives. This was a perfect imitation of the Elizabethan Poor Law invoking the principal of "primary family responsibility." In one historical exception—perhaps the first Massachusetts "welfare" law—the legislature voted to give relief to the refugees forced from their homes by King Phillip's War (1675). These were meager attempts at solving what was now a widespread problem.

Other solutions had included apprenticing or indenturing poor or orphaned children. This failed because it was clear that children could too easily be put into abusive situations, and also because the high birth rate left New England and the middle colonies with too many needy children.

In the 1730s, the other major colonial cities, Philadelphia and New York, also began to build almshouses. They wanted to house as many of the poor as possible under one roof. This was the beginning of a long trend toward substituting confinement in workhouses and almshouses for the older familial system of direct payments to the poor at home. The new system was designed to reduce the cost of care for a growing number of marginal persons. No longer was this group comprised of the aged, widowed, crippled, incurably ill, or orphaned members of society, but now included the seasonally unemployed, war veterans, new immigrants, and migrants from inland areas seeking employment in the cities.

Reports abounded about the squalor of the workhouses/almshouses, and the abuse of children within their walls. A step forward for welfare administration came with the adoption of the Massachusetts Constitution in 1794. It provided for a fully operational state government that centralized the passage and administration of Poor Laws. As the tumultuous century drew to a close, the Commonwealth of Massachusetts passed a bill creating "Workhouses for the Reception and Employment of the Idle and Indigent." The statute provided for the building of workhouses, the appointment of paid overseers to make regulations, and the requirement that towns buy the materials that those confined to the workhouse would need in order to be productive.

In 1794, the legislature also expanded the role of the overseers. They were now able to demand that family pay for poor relations, and to bind out the children of settlers who could not maintain them (as apprentices, servants, or any other type of labor). Similarly, adult strangers over the age of twenty-one could be bound out for one year. Finally, the law mandated emergency relief for anyone who fell into sudden distress.

This was the status of the Elizabethan Poor Laws, now nearly two hundred years old, as the new century dawned.

Children and Families in Puritan Massachusetts

The understanding and training of children was profoundly important to Puritan adults. The family, as a consequence, can truly be said to have been at the very center of the faith.

Preachers believed that children were "born evil." The catechism Reverend John Cotton prepared for the young of Massachusetts Bay Colony in 1646 included the following recitation: "I was conceived in sin, and born in iniquity....Adam's sin is imputed to me and a corrupt nature dwells within me." All adults believed that idleness in the young was particularly treacherous, and that the young were more likely to be idle, to be ungovernable. The Reverend Cotton Mather said, "For Satan finds some mischief still for idle hands to do." To keep those idle hands busy, children were expected to make productive use of every minute of their time. For example, children tending cattle and sheep were expected to spin thread or to weave while tending their flocks.

Parents in New England sought to tame children's natural tendencies to be "disobedient, stubborn, untractable, independent, contentious, insubordinate, rebellious, unwieldy, inflexible, obstinate, and proud." The anarchy they represented was a threat. Children had a place in the colonial world and were punished if they failed to keep their place.

To ensure that children understood their place, the leading ministers of the day recommended threatening children with eternal damnation. To bolster these sentiments, Massachusetts Bay adopted the *Body of Liberties* (1641) which prescribed capital punishment for children sixteen years or older who cursed or struck their natural mother or father. In 1648, the law was supplemented by saying that a disobedient or stubborn child could be brought to court and put to death. These same laws admonished parents to avoid "unnatural severitie" toward their children, *and* granted the children the right to complain to the authorities for redress.

However, this severe attitude toward the children in the family must be seen as parallel to the importance of the family itself. It was the primary social institution in the colonial period of American history. The family was, in effect, a comprehensive organic unit, a "little Commonwealth, and a little Church," the school that fit people to fulfill their religious and civic obligations. Common law had always taught that the duties of parents included maintaining and educating children during the seasons of infancy and youth. Under the common law, the father (and upon his death, the mother) was generally entitled to the custody of the infant children, because the parents were the children's natural protectors. Nevertheless, "when the morals, or safety, or interests of the children require it," the local government could intervene and "withdraw the infants from the custody of the father or mother and place the care and custody of them elsewhere." Society fully supported "intrusive" measures. Neighbors were encouraged to report those who worked on the Sabbath and who might be neglecting the needs of their children. Thus, there was no reported discontent when the selectmen of Watertown, after hearing complaints about families "under very needy and suffering circumstances," resolved that the town clerk should inform the families that they had to "put out" and "dispose of their children to such families where they might be taken good care of."

Here we can see the seeds of future American social policy and legal conflict being sown. No young people were ever put to death under the provisions of the stubborn child law, and there were no cases of children winning against their parents in court. However, these colonial laws betray powerful conflicting beliefs: beliefs in the supremacy of parental rights, in the supremacy of children's rights, and in the overriding concept of the state as *parens patriae* (the state as the parent or guardian).

CHAPTER TWO

THE ANTE-BELLUM ERA

1800–1860

CHAPTER TWO

The Ante-Bellum Era

1800–1860

"Every vacant spot behind, beside or within an old structure yielded room for still another. And eventually, to correct the oversight of the first builders who had failed to exhaust the ultimate inch, their more perspicacious successors squeezed house within house, exploiting the last iota of space. This resulted in so tangled a swarm that the compiler of the first Boston atlas gave up the attempt to map such areas, simply dismissed them as "full of sheds and shanties."

Oscar Handlin, describing dwelling places of the Irish immigrants, 1850 in *Boston's Immigrants*

PART ONE

Poverty

America in the decades leading up to the Civil War intensified the pattern laid down in the previous two centuries: exuberant growth of manufacturing and industry, and large waves of immigrants washing its shores. The century began with a population of 5,308,483 persons. Six million immigrants were added to the population in the next fifty years. Due to this immigration, and to natural increase, the population doubled every twenty-three years. If this doubling had continued, the nation would have passed the one billion mark in 1975! So great was the immigration that for a brief period in the early 1850s the foreign-born actually outnumbered the native born in Boston and New York. Boston's population in 1855 stood at 177,000, the fourth largest after New York, Philadelphia, and Baltimore.

Boston was not prepared for this influx of immigrants. The population of Massachusetts would increase by 36% between 1840 and 1860. By 1855, 50,000 Irish immigrants had immigrated to the city proper. Translated into percentages, in the first decade of the immigration, 1840 to 1850, the city's population grew by 90%, and in the second decade, 1850 to 1860, it grew by 75%. The school population increased 200%. One corner of the city recorded thirty-seven immigrants per dwelling.

Immigrants arriving in America in these years felt the effects of the financial panic that had hit in 1837 and that deepened into a lingering depression in the early 1840s. Common laborers and skilled craftsmen saw their jobs cut and wages reduced. Unprotected banks were nearly insolvent. The Irish entered the major ports of the East Coast with few skills and great need. They were willing to work at wages lower than those generally accepted by native workers. The only people who were not affected by the depression were the successful merchant-capitalists: the textile titans, their trading partners, and their banks. They had already contributed to the workingman's difficulties by replacing skilled craftsmen with machines. They could now advance further along the road of exploitation by hiring immigrants, whom they could squeeze with even lower wages than they had squeezed the native farm girls, their first wave of employees. In the last years of the depression, 1844–1845, eleven Lowell mills indicated dividends rising from 4.5% to 12.5%. The wages paid to the mill workers during this period were reduced from $2.00 per week to $1.75 per week.

Government Response

Exhibiting a total failure of imagination and a continuing indifference to the fate of the poor, Massachusetts opened the nineteenth century as it had closed the eighteenth—by building almshouses. Mayor of Boston Josiah Quincy II expressed a popular sentiment when he wrote in an 1821 report that he had carefully examined the cause of poverty and "discovered" that the perpetrators of poverty were the poor themselves! The poor, he said, "were like the vicious and criminal" who had no right to community maintenance. Their intemperance, their improvidence, was the cause of their pauperism. Too much charity merely encouraged them in their idle ways.

Quincy believed that of all the forms of aid, the most wasteful, the most expensive, the most injurious to morals and destructive of industrious habits, was that of "supply in their own families" (i.e., aiding them while they still lived in their own homes). "While they were with their families, they were indulged, as no work was demanded of them." He advocated the immediate end to outdoor relief, by which he meant relief outside of institutions. He said, "...the most economical mode is that of Alms House; having the character of Work Houses, or Houses of Industry, in which work is provided for every degree of ability in the pauper..." This, in spite of an earlier report to the state legislature that said, "The almshouse built in Boston in 1790 is, perhaps, the only instance known where persons of every description and disease are lodged under the same roof, and in some instances in the same contagious apartments; by which the sick are disturbed by noise of the healthy, and the infirm rendered liable to the vices and diseases of the diseased and profligate."

However, nothing deterred the building and use of almshouses. Massachusetts boasted 83 almshouses in 1824 and 219 in 1860. They were so popular as a means of dealing with the poor that by the end of the Civil War, four out of five persons in Massachusetts who received extended relief were in institutions.

Clergy Response

The opening decades of the nineteenth century witnessed yet another modification of Calvinism. The Congregational Church, the Massachusetts version of the old Puritan faith, altered the colonial view of man as predestined to condemnation, needing coercion to forego evil ways. The new Congregational Church believed that people had the power to change if properly led. The grim determinism of Calvinism was replaced by optimism; by dint of labor, Americans could prosper and banish the old European, class-driven poverty.

The Congregational Church underwent a friendly division in 1805 with the birth of the Unitarian Universalist Church. The leadership of this version was exceptionally literary and exceptionally philosophically oriented. The Massachusetts writers and educators who informed the intellectual life of New England in the first half of the nineteenth century were almost all Unitarians. Actual doctrinal differences with the Congregationalists were small. The significant difference lay in the sense of social activism among Unitarians. They became the forward movement of reform and they were in the lead when abolition of slavery began to stir the conscience of Boston. In light of this, the opinion espoused by William Ellery Channing, the most highly regarded Unitarian minister of his day, is especially disconcerting. He preached the following sermon to his parishioners in 1835:

> That some of the indigent die among us of scanty food, is undoubtedly true; but vastly more in this community die from eating too much, than from eating too little; vastly more from excess than from starvation. So as to clothing, many shiver from want of defenses against the cold; but there is vastly more suffering among the rich from absurd and criminal modes of dress...than among the poor from deficiency of raiment. Our daughters are oftener brought to the grave by their rich attire, than our beggar their nakedness. So the poor are often over

worked, but they suffer less than many among the rich, who have no work to do, no interesting objects to fill up life, to satisfy the infinite cravings of man for action. How many of our daughters are victims of ennui, a misery unknown to the poor, and more intolerable than the weariness of excessive toil.

This astonishing dismissal of genuine need was challenged by neither the civilian nor clergy leadership in Boston. Indeed, the legal establishment joined the clergy in supporting the hostile culture. Speaking to the graduating seniors at Harvard College in 1835, the widely respected Judge Theopholus Parsons firmly told the students that the masses must be taught that the rights of property were paramount and should not be undermined by labor movements. Historian Arthur Schlesinger, Jr. concluded, "The natural aristocracy of Massachusetts wheeled into action, intimidating opposition with the threat of ostracism and sabotaging any reform movement."

A prime exponent of the view that assistance to the poor put their souls in mortal jeopardy was Joseph Tuckerman, another leading Unitarian minister, who was much praised by Boston's leading citizens for his sacrifices in ministering to the poor! In 1835, he became the Secretary of the Association of Delegates from the Benevolent Societies of Boston. The Association consisted of twenty-six societies, including two infant schools and two that employed the female poor. In his first report, dated October 13, 1835, he explained that the goals of the Association of Benevolent Societies were to *avoid abuses in alms-giving* and to determine the most effective way to relieve the suffering of the poor. He further observed that the number of poor was increasing, that expenses were growing, and that in consequence they should be *helped with the least expenditure possible.* This could be achieved once it was understood that the policy of spending money on the poor was a mistake. "Now it is clear no great and permanent improvement of outward condition is to be looked for, but through an improvement of character; that the best resources for improving the condition of the poor are within themselves." (pp 7, 8 of Joseph Tuckerman's report to the Association of Delegates). (Emphasis is the author's.) Forty of the forty-eight-page pamphlet explained why spending money on the poor does nothing but expand their numbers. He noted that England had poor laws for over 200 years, yet the numbers of poor in England had greatly increased. Again, repeating the now-familiar theme, he claimed that giving alms takes away incentives to work, that the existence of systematic alms-giving perpetuates poverty, and that the givers and receivers of money should interact on a personal level so that gratitude can be properly expressed. When he was asked upon what principles the Association should act as distributors of alms, he answered that the principles consist of never giving alms to anyone who misrepresents his ability to work!

As the Financial Panic of 1837 deepened into the terrible depression of the early 1840s, the poor could expect nothing from the religious leadership to help fill their empty plates but self-serving bromides.

PART TWO

Children

The Family in Law; the Doctrine of Parens Patriae *(The State as Parent)*

The intrusiveness of the state, already described in chapter one, came from the religious belief that society was a collection of families rather than individuals. An individual who failed also failed his community. In the colonial world, the concept of *parens patriae* was so pervasive that it scarcely received comment. There was no challenge to the state's assumption of paternal, moral, or religious authority over the internal workings of the family.

These claims formed the basis of child-protection laws throughout the nineteenth and twentieth centuries. Puritanism's moral demands softened, but the importance of insuring the moral education of children, and the state's right to do so, did not.

An even more aggressive development of state power occurred during the first third of the nineteenth century. American courts expanded their authority to employ judicial discretion in deciding child custody disputes. Some courts, as early as the 1830s, declined to enforce the father's common-law prerogative and looked to the needs of the child. In determining the needs of a child, the court examined parental qualifications and asked, "Is this a nurturing parent?" Courts in Massachusetts were more conservative than others in the United States, stating that the father's automatically assumed common-law right to ownership and custody of his children could only be negated if he was of "grossly immoral" character and "wholly unable" to support the child. American courts varied from place to place, over the period, but they were steadily beginning to address issues that concern courts of our era: Are the claims of a mother and a father equal before the law? Should the age and gender of the child influence whether custody is awarded to a father or a mother? Should a child's preferences bear consideration, and if so, at what age? Merely asking the questions represented a softening of the common-law assumptions about paternal prerogatives and a quiet assertion that a child had separate rights.

Theories about children, rights of children

Changes in legal perceptions notwithstanding, nothing in the political life of America—neither the American Revolution, nor the creation of the Constitution, nor the incipient industrialization of the Commonwealth—altered the essential thinking about the nature of the child. The Puritanism of the founding fathers, always referred to more generically as "Calvinism," was now in its final incarnation, modified but still recognizable.

Seventeenth-century Calvinism, represented by Cotton Mather, had assumed that the newborn was wholly wicked. This doctrine of infant depravity led the Puritan parent to one simple task: to raise a child who would strictly obey the dictates of his parents and the demands of God. A person not raised to obey these two pillars of authority was a moral failure. He was depraved. The parent, equally, had failed God. There could be no greater failure.

Nineteenth-century Calvinism offered a somewhat kinder attitude toward children. The Reverend Timothy Dwight (1752-1817), grandson of Jonathan Edwards and longtime President of Yale, is an excellent example of the new Calvinism. Like most clergymen, he invoked the threat of hell for a job poorly done. Parents who loved their children raised them properly. Parents, therefore, were to blame for the unrestrained and unimproved child. This war against disorder was part of Dwight's well-ordered universe; all passions would be restrained, all laws would be obeyed. The gentler version of the doctrine came about with Dwight's admonition that love should surround the family. He wanted children to obey their parents out of love rather than fear.

Two other theories competed with reformed Calvinism in these decades. One had been proposed by John Locke, whose early eighteenth-century writings continued to influence American political theorists. In his highly-regarded *Essay Concerning Human Understanding*, he provided a striking counterpoint to the grim determinism of Calvinism. He wrote that the mind at birth is a blank slate. He said there was no original sin, and man was not born having to apologize for anything. Onto this *tabula rosa*, the parent imprinted the methods of rational thinking that would create the fulfilled and happy soul. However, nineteenth-century ministers applied the concept of the *tabula rosa* to rational faculties alone. The part of the soul that carried original sin was untouched.

Locke's writings were fundamental to the Enlightenment era in Europe. The Enlightenment triumphed over original sin by emphasizing the primacy of environmental influences in shaping individual character and conscience. The principle obligation of the parent was to produce a rational human being that could pursue happiness, a word singularly lacking in the Calvinist vocabulary.

Happiness was also a theme in the other intellectual response to Calvinism. It was called romanticism in Europe and transcendentalism in America. Romantics regarded the child as innately good, even morally superior to adults. The romantic child still had to attain eternal salvation, but he was born with the natural ability to do this. Romanticism may have had only limited application to child rearing, but it was useful to reformers: by sentimentalizing the child, romantics gave child advocates the tool they needed to rouse public opinion on the child's behalf.

Romantic theories were best expressed and applied by Bronson Alcott (1799-1888), transcendentalist, educator, and father of Louisa May Alcott. He raised his four daughters and directed a school according to the tenets of love first, faith second. He was too disorganized to be a financial success, but his theories managed to influence a small group of intellectuals and leaders, who gave New England a special color in the decades before the Civil War. Transcendentalists could not actually decide whether they preferred order or freedom, whether they idealized individualism or communalism, whether they wished people to be self-indulgent or ascetic. For Alcott, the happy child was not to be confused with the hedonistic child. Alcott taught that the main tenet of transcendental child-raising was to use gentle methods to promote ascetic ends. The lash of conscience should be ever-present, seldom discussed.

A leitmotif during these years was the question of whether or not the child was "just like an adult," but smaller (i.e., had the same thought processes), or was developmentally different. This concept has been alluded to above in the discussion of the changing attitudes of the courts. It was an important question for moral educators to address, since its answers had consequences for the penal statutes of the Commonwealth. The more conservative thinkers believed in full moral understanding and responsibility at a very young age. Children could be brought into court to answer for misdeeds at the age of seven (English common law) or ten (more enlightened American law). The reformers and educators introduced the idea of a gradual unfolding of the moral consciousness. They emphasized the importance of the environment in the education of the moral child.

The theories about the angelic nature of children—about the moment at which the child became a moral adult—were meant to apply to children of the middle and upper classes. They were irrelevant to the "ruffians" who roamed the streets of Boston, threatening the order that the middle and upper class cherished. The best solution the legislators and leaders could devise for dependent, neglected, and delinquent children (the three categories being interchangeable) was to put them in well-ordered institutions. Paralleling the growth of almshouses, these institutions spread rapidly through the country, from a handful in 1800 to 124 in 1860. Most of these "child saving institutions" were workhouses for children dependent on the state for care, institutions where children boarded for work, or less often, orphanages. At first, they were privately controlled by religious groups or by associations of national groups, but as the numbers of needy children grew, the state and city governments stepped up their efforts.

In 1826, the city of Boston became the first municipality in the country to build a reformatory for juveniles who had committed crimes. In 1835, a collaboration of the Unitarian Church and the state legislature built the Boston Asylum and Farm School, a home for "street Arabs," boys who existed by living on the street and committing petty crimes. Built on an island in Boston Harbor, its goal was to encourage agricultural as well as factory skills. In 1836, the Boston Friend Society received a charter to build an institution to house orphans and children surrendered by their parents. The legislation that chartered the school is typical of rehabilitation legislation of this period, emphasizing first and foremost that the children "shall be instructed in moral and religious duties and the branches of learning usually taught in the common town school," and describing the rules for their employment and apprenticeship.

The institutions were built for boys and girls alike to instill in them a sense of self-discipline, good morals, and Christian devotion. The quality of the institutions varied. Some actually succeeded in teaching a trade and bringing a sense of order to children's lives. Overseers who seemed to specialize in sadism supervised others. There is the diary of one such overseer, described by historian David Rothman, who recorded daily the number of boys whom he had subjected to whippings, leg irons, solitary confinement, handcuffs, and ball and chain.

A glimpse of a more promising future for children dawned in Massachusetts in 1863 when Charles Birtwell, an exceptionally visionary reformer, formed the Boston Children's Aid Society. He and his colleagues were appalled to learn that children as young as ten years old sat in jail alone for days in court-ordered silence while awaiting trial. They began by simply sitting with the children. Subsequently, they founded their own school for wayward youth. The school, Pine Farm, successfully housed and schooled boys for twenty years. The workers became their legal guardians, keeping the boys at the farm or binding them out to permanent homes in the country. Birtwell encouraged his staff to remain in touch with the parents of the boys. The guardians became personal probation officers, taking responsibility for the boys following court orders. The society's entire emphasis was on the needs of the individual child. It explored the concept of "foster homes" and wrote a guide on how to investigate a potential home and how to evaluate the placement. Unfortunately, Pine Farm and Charles Birtwell were ahead of their time. In spite of the nationwide movement, led in part by Massachusetts reformers, to remove every last child from every last almshouse by 1900, the 1880s and 1890s continued to see Massachusetts pass laws mandating that all poor and indigent children between the ages of three and sixteen be committed by the State Board of Health, Lunacy, and Charity to either a state-sponsored primary school (in reality, a reform school) or the state almshouse.

Children and work, 1800–1860

Alexander Hamilton had advised in his 1791 *Report on Manufactures* that industry employ children to work the machines because small hands were more adept at operations and employers could pay children lower wages. When Samuel Slater opened his groundbreaking cotton-spinning mill in Pawtucket, Rhode Island, he followed Hamilton's advice: his work force consisted entirely of children.

Children had always been an integrated part of a farm family's economic unit, doing farm work or helping their mothers with domestic chores, such as spinning and weaving. Therefore, it was not a sudden leap into the unknown to employ them in factories. However, as the demand for easily exploited labor grew and the poverty of the immigrant population intensified, it was inevitable that factories would employ increasing numbers of children. Employers chose to ignore the danger and tedium of factory life. It was assumed that children would work adult hours, typically twelve hours a day. Rules about breaks during the day were rigid and punishment severe. Contrast this with the few hours they might work with a hoe in the company of siblings, or with a sewing project in the front parlor that all the girls would attend to as they found the time. Work in a nineteenth-century factory takes on a different, darker meaning.

Massachusetts passed its first regulatory laws with regard to children in 1824, attempting to increase factory safety and reduce the length of the workday. These laws were ignored. However, at least one law was enforced, a law passed in 1842 saying that said no child under the age of twelve could work more than ten hours a day. Regulating work encouraged the more reform-minded lawmakers to think about public school education. The Massachusetts legislature passed a "first in the nation" compulsory school attendance law in 1855, declaring that no child under the age of fifteen could be employed in a manufacturing establishment who had not attended school for eleven weeks a year, including the eleven weeks just prior to his employment.

Children and education

A literate child, female as well as male, was a goal of the Calvinist clergy. New Englanders in general were always credited with having an unusually high literacy rate. Harvard College was a critically important cultural icon in Massachusetts and it required an infrastructure of preparatory schools. The early movement for free public elementary school is usually credited to Massachusetts. A historian writing in 1826 about Boston schools pronounced them "exemplary." The system was comprised of fifty-one primary schools, nineteen grammar schools, one school for blacks, two boys' high schools, and the country's first high school for girls.

However public support for public education weakened from the moment it began. The Protestant elite were already sending their children to private schools and had no interest in funding public ones. Further, the captains of industry and the parents of the children in question both wanted the children to go to work. As a result, public school attendance in the first half of the 19th century remained small.

The foremost champion of universal public education was a secular minister, Horace Mann. He believed that everything good and desirable in civic life could be attained with an educated citizenry. Horrified at the political turmoil in Europe of 1848, he fervently believed that an educated citizenry was the last best hope for democracy, the most effective hedge against despotism and social unrest. Education would defeat the class rigidity that plagued Europe. And, he would add, education produced those very character traits that material success in a market-oriented economy required: punctuality, cheerful obedience, honesty, responsibility, perseverance, and farsightedness.

Eventually, Mann and his fellow reformers made progress. By the 1850s, Massachusetts had acquired all the essentials of a modern educational establishment: special "normal schools" for the training of female teachers, uniform textbooks, a uniform system of grading and advancing students, and an administrative bureaucracy for supervising the system. Although the children of the very poor continued to avoid school, the movement for universal, compulsory, free public education was gaining ground among all classes. In time, every young child's life would be touched by it. In time, education would be understood to be an exit from poverty.

CHAPTER THREE

THE GILDED AGE

1865–1900

CHAPTER THREE

The Gilded Age

1865–1900

Introduction

Beginning with the Civil War, and accelerating in the years afterward, the United States' growth as an industrial giant was without parallel in the world. The country possessed the labor (augmented by a large, steady immigrant stream), the natural resources, endless seams of coal and iron ore, and the audacious enterprise of bold men—uninhibited by government regulations or personal morals.

Government appeared, to the nation and to the men themselves, to exist solely to assist them in their vast undertakings. The exchange of generous bribes to legislators for munificent gifts of land and other necessities led to such observations as that made by Henry Demarest Lloyd, that John D. Rockefeller "had done everything to the Pennsylvania legislature except refine it."

Before the century was over, America counted more than four thousand millionaires among its citizens. The unrestrained accumulation of untaxed wealth led to excesses in spending unimaginable at any other time. Cornelius Vanderbilt built and furnished his Newport mansion for $11 million. The parties that the Vanderbilts gave saw men smoking cigars rolled up $100 bills. The guests were provided with sterling silver pails and shovels with which to dig for rubies, sapphires, and diamonds. Their horse stalls were lined with linen sheets embossed with the family monogram.

Thus, the Gilded Age.[1]

While Vanderbilt and his friends were cavorting at Newport, 10 million immigrants were landing on the East Coast of the United States. The immigrants came from poverty and landed in poverty. They were willing to work at any job that was available, but work was not always available. Between 1873 and 1893, the country cycled through four financial panics and/or economic depressions. Both the native farm population and the urban immigrant population were strongly affected by these crises.

The farmers, finding that they could not get assistance from the two major parties, formed the Populist Party. It did not succeed on the national stage, partly because its leaders and platform did not address the city and its needs. The immigrants, with very limited English and no protection against urban predators, turned to the urban boss. The cities were swollen beyond imagining. By 1900, three cities housed a population of over one million.

The American people, in general, continued to be hostile to anyone asking for help. They could not believe that a man who became unemployed because of a business depression was a man whose family deserved aid. They could not accept the reality of a man going from town to town searching for work. Men (or families) who traveled stood in real danger of being branded as tramps. The judgment of "tramp" in Massachusetts (echoing the earlier "stranger" designation) meant a sentence of six months to two years in a house of correction.

The American people also remained hostile to those who struck for better wages and safer working conditions. The owners of the coal mines and steel factories also controlled the newspapers. Citizens either did not know or did

---

1 The name became popular after Mark Twain titled his novel about the era, *The Gilded Age*.

not want to know about the brutal conditions under which these men worked. All the newspaper had to do was label the strikers as "communists" or "reds," and the public supported violent strikebreaking by private police or government troops.

The general public's hostility to labor grievances and the woes of the unemployed was greatly enhanced by Social Darwinism, the guiding philosophy of the Gilded Age. In *Origin of Species*, Charles Darwin postulated that plant and animal life was a fierce and unrelenting struggle for survival. The misinterpretation of Darwin's evolutionary theory as simply the "survival of the fittest" (i.e., "most prosperous") was the perfect companion and the scientific justification for the Calvinist belief that the separation between the successful rich and the despised poor was part of a divine plan.

The decade of the nineties—the "Gay Nineties"—witnessed a fierce four-year depression. The depression of 1893-1897 was longer and deadlier than any America had experienced to that time. Major banks and railroad companies failed. By the end of 1893, 16,000 businesses had closed their doors. The number of unemployed grew to fearsome levels. Organized charity, until now firmly committed to denying even one cent to the poor, lest a hideous dependency be developed, relented. The New York Department of Charities and Correction gave direct aid to the blind and free coal to the poor. Josephine Shaw Lowell, its general secretary, reversed decades of rhetoric condemning the poor, when she wrote that the plight of the poor was "not due usually to moral or intellectual defects on their own part, but to economic causes over which they could have no control, and which were as much beyond their power to avert as if they had been natural calamities of fire, flood, or storm."

The depression seemed to give the poor the human identity they had previously lacked. In 1907, Edwin T. Devine, national editor of the journal *Charities*, wrote, "We might quite safely throw overboard, once and for all, the idea that the dependent poor are our moral inferiors, that there is any necessary connection between wealth and virtue, or between poverty and guilt."

Those were heart-warming sentiments for those seeking to turn the poor from strangers into real people. They were, however, in the history of American alms-giving, ahead of its time. .

PART ONE

Immigrants and organized charity

Once again, the story begins with immigrants and the mixed response of the American public: "Yes, we need your labor. No, we don't like you, so keep yourselves out of our sight."

Between 1870 and 1900, 10 million immigrants from southern and eastern Europe poured into the cities of the East Coast of the United States. Their ships docked in the big city ports, and that's where they remained for the most part. The cities—Boston, New York, Philadelphia, Baltimore—were neither prepared nor welcoming.

That is not to say that America had no use for all its newcomers. In the years before the Civil War, America was judged a second-rate industrial country, certainly behind Great Britain, France, and Germany. By 1900, the muscle and sweat of its immigrant labor force had produced a towering industrial giant, with manufactured goods now seen as equal in value to the combined production of the three former leading countries.

The immigrants lived where they worked. Their cities grew without plan or design. Urban planning was a concept not yet born. In its place, greed was the ruling principle. Greed produced the tenement and the slum. The basic idea was to herd as many people into as many subdivided cubicles as possible, and to charge each one of them rent. Residential congestion in American cities at the end of the nineteenth century was greater than anywhere else in the world. In Chicago, home to European immigrants and newly-urban southern blacks, hundreds of houses were not connected to sewers. In New York City's densest ward, there were 1,000 people per acre, over 300,000 per square mile. In Boston, a substantial portion of the immigrant population was housed in basements and subbasements with no windows. Only vermin had previously enjoyed such living quarters. Disease and despair ruled.

Government in the nineteenth century followed in the footsteps of government in the eighteenth and seventeenth centuries; it would consider no laws that "interfered" with the lives of private citizens, following the maxim that "government is best which governs least." Private citizens, unless they were financial titans seeking millions for grand adventures in railroads, did not ask for or expect government assistance. This meant that as this period of intense industrialization began, there were no health and safety regulations, no limitations on daily or weekly work hours (in a typical factory, sixty to eighty hours a week, seven days a week was the norm), no unemployment or disability insurance, no aid to dependent children, no old age security, or government-sponsored medical care. The total absence of government assistance coupled with a cycle of financial panics and depressions every ten years between 1873 and 1893 produced glimmers of limited activity in the private sector. The first organized charity movement was born.

The *organized* charities began on the state level in Boston in 1869 with the founding of the Boston Associated Charities. The movement became a widespread national organization in 1874 with the creation of the National Conference of Charities and Correction.

"Organized" was the word the charities were proud of, because it conveyed to the public that the charity had entered into the scientific age. Instead of random, disorganized giving in which *a poor person might apply for and receive aid more than once*, or, less tolerable, that *an undeserving person* might receive aid, scientific charity (its practitioners preferred the name, *scientific philanthropy*) promised no undeserved aid. In fact, it promised no aid at all. The charity organizations promised only that they would maintain lists of applicants and collect information about the poor. Inspired, perhaps, by the clerical leadership of the preceding generation, every charity agency was, as this era opened, committed to *withholding* cash relief. The fear of giving cash relief continued unabated. Stated simply and repetitively, cash relief contributed to the moral degeneracy of the poor. This "outdoor relief" would give them an incentive NOT to work; if they did not work, they would be committing the sin of voluntary *pauperism*. Pauperism was a terrible disease in which a person preferred sloth over work, preferred begging over earning his way. Boston Associated Charities had stated its goal: it would refuse to give cash assistance and in so doing would prevent the next generation of paupers. Amos G. Warner, the general agent for the Charity Organization Society of Baltimore, wrote that unemployment and illness were responsible for almost half of the poverty cases, but that a significant cause in the remaining half was "unwise philanthropy" (cash handouts). The latter fostered "indolence," "lubricity," and a variety of "unhealthy appetites."

The ideal of scientific philanthropy, instead of indiscriminate cash distribution, was to help the individual through example and precept, through sympathy and encouragement of personal relations. The person who would do this was called the "Friendly Visitor." This Friendly Visitor to the poor became the focal point of the entire effort, the sole justification for the complex machinery of scientific benevolence.

It was the personal relationship between the giver and the recipient that differentiated benevolence from mere alms-giving. This personal relationship required a careful investigation. Critics said "investigation" only succeeded in pinning a label on the client. Advocates said that it was analogous to a physician's diagnosis; it was essential to gather information before providing the appropriate prescription.

The organized charity movement believed that effective charity was a process not of social reform, but of character regeneration. Its practitioners were successful, educated, and cultured representatives of the upper and middle classes, people who benefited from the status quo. As such, they could only conclude that the failures of poor families were not structural (lack of employment), but personal (unwillingness to work). The Friendly Visitor's task was to ascertain the cause of the failure and give the necessary advice to fix it. With these assumptions in mind, the Friendly Visitor did not apologize for her intrusion into the family home. She believed she was helping when she asked questions to determine the cause of the moral lapse, and then offered herself as the person whose example and friendship would save the family from doom.

The friendly visiting movement could not be sustained. To begin with, it was extremely labor intensive. Each Friendly Visitor was supposed to work with only three or four families. By 1900, Boston, the leader of the movement, was struggling to keep a roster of 1,000 volunteers, but no other city came near that number. Baltimore was more typical, with 150.

However, there was a far more profound reason for its failure. The very concept of a friendship between non-equals was doomed. The visitors were mostly women, entirely English-speaking, Protestant, and wealthy. The immigrants were Catholic, spoke little or no English, and could not see the point of an intrusive visitor who might make sympathetic noises about their poverty but refuse cash help. The charity agents protested that they came to offer something more important than cash—friendship, role-modeling, and character reform. The recipients of this noblesse oblige could be forgiven if they saw the visitors simply as people who thought that a clean floor was more important than a full larder, implying all the while that they would be less poor if they were more moral.

At this point in American history, we can begin, slowly but confidently, to bury the concept of the "scientific charity."

It is true that the societies had not been entirely passive recorders of misery and dispensers of high-minded advice. Some of them engaged in a small amount of job training. There were several established day nurseries for working mothers. A few got involved in the movement for public kindergartens. Organized charity in Poughkeepsie, New York, helped to develop kitchen gardens. Reverend Robert Treat Paine, President of Boston Associated Charities for twenty-eight years, started a small-loan association for beginning businesses, capitalized with his own money. Charity organizations in Baltimore and New York followed his example. Toward the end of the nineteenth century, in a break with the tradition of dismissing the role of government, Reverend Paine lobbied the city of Boston to improve sanitation and to regulate the building of housing for the poor.

The foregoing notwithstanding, "scientific charity" is consigned by historians to an unwelcome corner of American history: the last gasp of Calvinism, whose ideals created an appropriate distance between the prosperity of the "elect" and the disease of the afflicted pauper.

Settlement Houses

Much to the good fortune of the immigrant poor in the nineteenth century, succor did not stop at the door of the obsessively record-keeping charities.

In Chicago, a young woman newly returned from an investigatory trip to England, moved into a run-down house on a dirty street in a very disagreeable part of town. The year was 1889. The young woman was Jane Addams, and she had just established Hull House, soon to become America's most famous settlement house.

Ms. Addams and her fellow workers took up residence in Hull House. They did not enter people's homes and they did not pose intrusive questions. They asked, "How can we help you?" They offered services. The settlement house workers did not assume that the immigrant family was a dysfunctional unit within a smoothly functioning society. They perceived instead that immigrant families were functioning families overwhelmed by forces beyond their control. In a departure from 250 years of American history, they did not try to distinguish between the worthy and the unworthy poor. The settlement house movement was a long overdue bow in the direction of the human beings that found themselves helplessly at the bottom rung of the new industrial age.

The founding of the settlement houses coincided with the early years of the progressive movement. Government was not to be ignored; it was to be *reformed*. Before long the Hull House workers were involved in campaigns for municipal reform. Jane Addams herself took on the powerful and very corrupt alderman, Johnny Powers. She lived in the center of his impoverished ward; she observed the uncollected garbage strewn on the street. Addams applied for and received an appointment as garbage inspector. She rose at six every morning and in a horse-drawn buggy followed the infuriated garbage contractor on his appointed rounds, making sure every receptacle was emptied. Powers was furious. Garbage inspection was one of the many jobs reserved for his political henchmen. This was, however, the only victory she was to be permitted. Over the years, she and her colleagues repeatedly challenged his position as alderman; each time they thought they had the votes to win, but they never did. He always bought the voters and the vote counters. Johnny Powers successfully fought reform candidates until his death in 1930. But Hull House and its resident workers went on to play leadership roles in the great social movements of the early twentieth century.

Hull House and its 400 sister settlement houses offered nurseries, club rooms, kindergartens, maintenance of playgrounds, rooms for bathing and showering, English classes, nutrition and hygiene classes, help in navigating the education and legal systems, and anything else the bewildered immigrant might need.

Further, the settlement houses provided an unparalleled education to the young middle-class workers who resided there. A stunning group of young women emerged. They were at the forefront of Progressive Era legislation, became the visionaries who founded the first schools of social work, and were responsible for the research that overturned Supreme Court rulings. They elected from their ranks the first woman to sit in Congress and the first woman to be appointed to a cabinet post. The list includes: Hull House graduates Julia Clifford Lathrop, who took up residence directly after her graduation from Wellesley College and worked to establish the first fully-accredited juvenile court in the United States (Chicago, Illinois, 1899); Florence Kelley, who wrote the first factory inspection law in the nation and then became the first factory inspector of Chicago sweatshops and founder of the National Consumers League (she was known to friends and adversaries alike as a "human volcano"); Dr. Alice Hamilton, who developed the first well-baby clinic in Chicago, went on to develop clinics for children in Boston, and finally became a pioneer in industrial medicine; and Grace Abbott, who became director of the Immigrants' Protective League, and, as staff member of the newly-established federal Children's Bureau, wrote clauses prohibiting child labor in all government war contracts during World War I. Henry Street Settlement House founder Lillian Wald taught nursing to immigrant women and helped found the New York Visiting Nurses Association. Another Henry Street graduate, Francis Perkins, became the Secretary of Labor in New York State and the first woman to occupy a post in the cabinet of the federal government, appointed by Franklin D. Roosevelt to be his Secretary of Labor. Other Settlement House leaders were leaders in the fight against child labor, for aggressive boards of health, for compulsory school attendance, and, above all, for municipal government reform. In this work, they leant professionalism to social work and validation to the needs of the poor. They were the advanced guard of the assault on government's resistance to helping the needy.

PART TWO

Children in the Gilded Age

The care of destitute, neglected, and delinquent children entered a new phase in the last quarter of the nineteenth century. From the time of the country's founding, destitute children were usually housed with the adult poor in almshouses and workhouses. The best a child could hope for was to be housed separately from the insane and criminal adult population. For over 200 hundred years, reformers beseeched their fellow citizens in vain about the abuses of these institutions. Gradually, states began passing laws mandating separation of children from adults and, by 1872, most states had done so. Nonetheless, the United States census report of 1890 revealed that 7,250 children aged zero to twenty were housed in almshouses and workhouses (virtually synonymous concepts) indiscriminately with adults. Of these, 2,555 were under five years old.

The most interesting and aggressive experiment in child placement of this era took place in New York in a slum that was arguably the worst in the nation. The "Five Points" section of the city was home to rats and filth, to every corruption known to man, and to young boys who slept every night of their lives on the street. Charles Loring Brace was a young minister newly returned from observing homes for delinquent children in England and Germany. He worked with police officers and businessmen to create the Children's Aid Society (CAS). At first, the CAS created the usual programs: evening schools, sheltered workshops, industrial education classes for the boys, sewing machine training schools for the girls, lodging houses for newsboys and bootblacks, and penny savings banks. The society had the commonly delineated mixed goals of helping the needy, combating juvenile crime, and promulgating Christian moral uplift.

Brace was persuaded that these reforms were futile. He believed that street urchins could not be saved in the unwholesome, poisonous environment of the city. Further, he shared a very popular idea of that time, "the agrarian myth." Simply stated, "If it happens on the farms of America, it is morally superior." CAS began to place urban children with rural families. The project began in 1854 with a train trip of forty-six boys and girls to a small town in Michigan, and ended in 1921 with a shipment of three boys to Texas. Over a period of sixty-seven years, the organization relocated more than 100,000 youngsters.

It is difficult to evaluate a project as large as the "Orphan Train." Brace's program ran for sixty-seven years, outliving its founder. A hundred thousand or more children were placed in tens of thousands of homes all across the Midwest and Southwest. Interviews with some of the children still alive today and letters published at various times throughout this century reflect a range of responses to this program: from deep gratitude to anger to a barely coherent longing for something that was missed, though the author does not know what. The program did have some inherent flaws. It did not carefully distinguish between the orphaned and the merely poor. Some parents and children were deceived into thinking they would see each other again, when in fact they would not. There was also no way to perform a quality evaluation of the receiving homes or count the number of boys and girls who "succeeded" and who "failed." The Catholic Church correctly pointed out that a Protestant Society had taken mainly Catholic children and placed them to be raised in homes that were almost entirely Protestant. The program also ran into opposition when the receiving states began to complain that they needed placements for their own poor children.

The flaws notwithstanding, this child-saving mission had more plusses than minuses. When Brace first put his plan into action, he alone in the field of child welfare insisted that the child's needs came first; punishment, if necessary, came last. In the city, he began as a one-man show, attending to thousands of children who otherwise would have spent every day of their short lives on the street. Not only the children, but the nation as a whole benefited. At least two governors and a host of good citizens emerged from this program. This is a balance sheet in which the good appears to outweigh the bad.

Another child-placement institution in nineteenth-century America was the orphanage. From 1727, when King Louis XIV established the Ursuline Convent Orphanage in New Orleans, until the mid-twentieth-century, orphanages have played an important role in child placement. In colonial days, children orphaned by Indian attacks or epidemics of disease, such as cholera and yellow fever, were housed in orphanages. From the 1830s to the 1840s, orphan asylums, typically run by churches, were considered the best way to care for these children. After the Civil War, most children in orphanages were not full but half orphans, or children living with one parent. But many had two parents whose illness or temporary poverty made it impossible to keep their children at home. The majority would be placed temporarily, eventually returning to their families. Religious groups continued to be the primary organizers of orphanages. This made the churches exceptionally popular among the immigrant poor.

The need for orphanages was greatly reduced by the introduction of New Deal programs like widows' pensions and unemployment insurance. Although the orphanages are now shuttered and closed, disappointment with the current foster-care system and other available institutions has produced a resurrection of the idea of the orphanage as an alternative for child placement.

Orphanages kept siblings together, enabled parents to place them and take them home again without any ruling from a judge, and gave the children a sense of belonging to a community where everyone was more or less in the same situation. However, a modern day orphanage would be prohibitively expensive to administer; it would also be burdened with a highly unsavory reputation. It is very unlikely that one will be built, or, if it were built, that it would be used.

The First "Protection" Policy

The Children's Aid Society had a quiet counterpart that was to grow in strength over the years. In 1875, the Society for the Prevention of Cruelty to Children (SPCC) began to address the problem of child abuse within families. The dramatic story of the beginning of the SPCC begins in a New York courtroom. A volunteer social worker found that no agency was willing to intervene on behalf of a neglected and abused ten-year-old girl who was living with her stepmother. In desperation, the social worker turned to the Society for the Prevention of Cruelty to Animals, insisting that a human child was also a member of the animal species. The attorney for the SPCA and the social worker arranged to have the child brought to court. The judge placed the child in the temporary care of the SPCA, which arranged for a foster home. With the help of the SPCA's general counsel, a new agency, the SPCC, was born. A nineteenth-century historian observed that, "It is a singular fact that the organized protection of abused children grew out of the organized protection of abused animals."

Education

Recall that in 1855, Massachusetts passed a compulsory school attendance law. It was a failure. Abundant evidence from every urban center of the country demonstrated that the children of the poor worked; they did not go to school. Case studies of Massachusetts working-class families conducted in 1875 provided the explanation: unskilled male laborers could supply only two-thirds of a family's needs for survival; their wives and children supplied the other third. The labor of children under the age of fifteen paid for 20% of poor families' expenditures.

The Massachusetts legislature tried again in 1898, ordering all cities and towns to provide schooling for thirty-two weeks a year. Every town of 500 was to maintain an adequately equipped high school, and cities of 10,000 or more had to maintain evening high schools. The parents of truants could be fined for their children's failure to obey school attendance laws. But the economic realities did not change.

For the next fifty years, education reformers played a tug-of-war game against an alliance of factory owners and impoverished parents. Until and unless poor parents could earn a more reliable income, and until and unless the legislatures could be convinced to limit children's working hours in factories, compulsory school attendance laws would continue to fail. The children's lives, and the lives of their parents, were now in the hands of the crusading reformers whose unseen work would make the progressive era the beginning of the end of their exploitation.

CHAPTER FOUR

THE PROGRESSIVE ERA AND BEYOND

1900–1930

CHAPTER FOUR

The Progressive Era and Beyond

1900–1920

Introduction

The Gilded Age had devoted itself to creating wealth.

The next generation, profoundly disturbed by the recklessness, violence, and disorder of the Gilded Age, began to calculate the social costs of rapid and untrammeled industrial growth and material prosperity. Social critic Herbert Croly observed that the American people had to be emancipated from the "energetic and selfish individualism that pervaded the recent past." He and his fellow critics argued that the federal government would have to assume a major responsibility. They envisioned an enlightened, strengthened regulatory state that utilized professional expertise and social planning.

Progressive leaders believed that the "best men" should govern. These men would be educated in political and economic theory and would be able to improve society with their knowledge of "scientific management." Progressive Christianity supported the reformers, claiming that the "regeneration of a society can come only through the act of God, and God is now acting." Many small town businessmen supported progressivism because the large banks, the conglomerated railroads, and the corrupt business practices encouraged by big city bosses hurt small businessmen and their banks.

President Theodore Roosevelt became the dynamic leader without whose vision and support many reforms would have failed. During his presidency, Roosevelt was directly responsible for the passage of the Pure Food and Drug Act, the Forest Reserve Act, the regulation of railroad rates under the Interstate Commerce Commission, the Elkins Act, and the Hepburn Act. He provided excellent leadership for the crusaders for children's rights, calling the first White House Conference on Children.

In his quest for order and "responsible" government, Roosevelt urged Congress to agree upon workmen's compensation and child labor laws, a railway hour act, income and inheritance taxes, and a law prohibiting corporations from contributing to political parties. When the federal courts used the power of injunction to prevent labor unions from striking, he turned angrily against the courts, calling for recall of judicial decisions. Under federal leadership, the comprehensive New York City Tenement House Law of 1901 was passed. It required that buildings guarantee light and circulation of air, and that inspectors monitor the quality of building materials.

The Progressive reformers, turning to juvenile law and protection, had a significant influence on children's lives. State legislation was passed to control child labor, compel school attendance, and create separate juvenile courts. The separate juvenile court system required its own personnel for monitoring the children brought before it, so a corps of probation officers grew, along with the court. The probation officers became a cadre of "court social workers," focusing on the child's needs.

Regrettably, to a large extent the Supreme Court effectively put a brake on Progressive legislation. The Progressive agenda created turmoil in Congress. After heated debate, a law limiting child labor was passed. It relied on the use of the Interstate Commerce Commission and the taxing powers of Congress. This law and others were frustrated by a group of activist conservative justices who tenaciously defeated, by judicial proclamation, what the legislators had struggled to create in the elected assemblies. Genuine statutory change would only occur under the auspices of a Supreme Court with a different membership.

Children during the Progressive Era

Child Saving, Child Protection

Of all the social ills that fueled the progressive impulse, none stirred the reforming zeal more than the problems of children. In 1909, President Theodore Roosevelt called a White House Conference on Dependent Children, which was attended by 200 prominent men and women from all over the country. It brought the plight of dependent children before the entire nation and gave to social work, especially child welfare, a new and prominent place in national life. The conference was an expression of the slow erosion of the long-held belief that government was not responsible for the nation's social welfare.

The gathering had two tasks: to encourage the exchange of ideas and experiences among leading advocates for dependent children and to create a general plan for their care. The final report was a forceful indictment of those remaining charity workers who still preferred to remove children from their homes. "Home life," the report proclaimed, "is the highest and finest product of civilization. Children should not be deprived of it except for urgent and compelling reasons." For those children "who for sufficient reasons must be removed from their homes, or who have no homes, it is desirable that they should be cared for in families whenever practicable. The carefully selected foster home is for the normal child the best substitute for the natural home."

The progressive impulse was to counter the nineteenth-century reflexive habit of removing children from their homes; Progressives felt, justifiably, that too much class bias was involved in the decision to remove. This report, however, merely papered over a conflict that child advocates have yet to resolve: what policy serves the welfare of a child best? Is it continued placement with the biological family, assuming the family situation can be improved? Or is it placement outside the family, assuming the placement is an improvement over existing conditions? These questions, provoked by this report, were to be recycled repeatedly throughout the twentieth century.

One of the most immediate and important results of this conference was the creation of the U.S. Children's Bureau. Settlement House leaders had proposed the idea repeatedly, but business always violently opposed it, fearful that a bureau would lead to the end of child labor. During the five days of bitter debate that accompanied the bill this time, Congress charged that those who favored the Children's Bureau were working under orders from European socialists and communists, who intended to use the agency to regulate the nation's youth. After three years of struggle, the bill was passed and signed into law by President Howard Taft on April 9, 1912. Immediately, Taft appointed Julia Lathrop, a former Hull House resident *and* a member of the Illinois State Board of Charities as its head. Lathrope became the first woman to lead a federal agency.

The Bureau commenced its important work of investigating and reporting on all matters pertaining to the welfare of children. Their data was trusted and was used repeatedly when any related issues were argued. The Bureau's major investigation, of America's infant mortality rate, revealed shockingly high numbers. Inadequate family income and inadequate medical facilities were cited as the two primary causes. The study also revealed that the maternal death rate was higher in America than in any other leading nation in the world. This led Julia Lathrop, in 1916, to write a piece of legislation called the Comprehensive Infancy and Maternity Bill. Representative Jeanette Rankin of Montana, the first woman to serve in the House of Representatives, presented it to Congress. It became known as the Sheppard-Towner Bill (for the names of its sponsors). The bill called for federal funding of clinics in which (mostly) nurses would administer the care. It would be fair to describe the medical profession as "hysterical." It did not stop with the usual epithets of "socialist" and "communist." Organized medicine manipulated every conceivable lobbying tactic to work against the bill's provision for clinics in poor areas, calling it state medicine.

Typical of the attacks on the bill was a pamphlet written by the Illinois State Medical Society entitled, *Shall the Children of America Become the Property of the State?* It reviled the Children's Bureau, whose leaders were referred to as "endocrine perverts [and] derailed menopausics, masquerading as humanity" while "battening upon the incredulous imagination of the citizens who feel that by this legislation they might evade some of their responsibilities....*The Children's Bureau will by this bill be the ruling power in the United States. This bureau, headed by one woman, will become the most despotic influence in the country, imposing a yoke that will annually become more unbearable in its crushing burdens.*" (Emphasis is the author's.) Finally, in a rhetorical flourish unmatched in the Senate in this century, Thomas Reed of Missouri warned that if the Sheppard-Towner bill passed, "female celibates would instruct mothers on how to bring up their babies."

After three years of floor debate, during which hurling vile epithets at prominent women leaders became standard behavior, President Warren G. Harding signed the bill into law on November 9, 1921. The act provided funds for public-health nurses to teach parents how to care for their children. It established nearly 3,000 rural clinics in forty-five states where children could be examined while their mothers attended classes on nutrition and sanitation. In addition, the act strengthened state health departments and helped foster the development of county health units, which in turn led to the better administration of local services. In the eight years of the law's existence, the nation saw a significant drop in infant and maternal mortality. Congress, pleased to bow to the fierce lobbying of the American Medical Association, allowed Sheppard-Towner to expire in 1929. The rural clinics had had far too much medical care supplied by nurses and midwives. The improvements they made to women's and infants' health were deemed irrelevant.

Child Labor, Child Education

The progressive crusade to eliminate child labor captured public opinion. It never suffered from the outrageous, insulting rhetoric that greeted nursing care for women and children. The public understood that industrial work bore no relationship to the kind of character-building farm chores that children did to help secure the family income. Angry reporters, such as John Spargo[2], brought this home to the reading public.

At the turn of the century, one out of six children was gainfully employed, two million between the ages of ten and fifteen. No one knows how many children under the age of ten worked, and data is lacking altogether for white and

---

[2] In *Bitter Cry of the Children*, Spargo wrote, "The boys sat for ten or eleven hours a day in rows on wooden boards placed over chutes through which tons of coal constantly passed. Their task was to pick out from the passing coal the slate, stone and other waste that came from the mine. The slate so closely resembled the coal that it could be detected only by close scrutiny. The boys had to bend over the chute and reach down into it...the moving material was so sharp it tore their hands. If a boy reached too far and slipped into the coal that flowed beneath him, he stood little chance of surviving intact. Boys of ten and twelve do this work for ten hours a day earning fifty or sixty cents."

black children working on rural farms. It was estimated that other people's parents employed 60% of the children who worked on farms. Others worked in cotton, woolen, and silk mills, in clothing and tobacco sweatshops, in coal and iron mills, and up to 2.5 million in street trades.

In 1902, Lillian Wald, leader of the New York City Henry Street Settlement House, and Florence Kelley, graduate of Hull House, assembled representatives of thirty-two settlement houses in New York City to discuss child labor. The result was the formation in 1904 of the National Child Labor Committee. Its first success was a law passed in New York that outlawed children's work in street trades. By 1907, two-thirds of the states had either initiated legislation regulating children's work or greatly improved and strengthened their existing laws.

In 1912, the Children's Bureau, now a permanent part of the Department of Commerce and Labor, set forth its agenda on child labor: a minimum work age of fourteen in manufacturing and sixteen in mining, an eight-hour day, and prohibition of night work. By 1914, forty-seven states had minimum age limits for working children. A majority of the states prohibited children from working in highly dangerous occupations, and over half forbade night work under a specified age. A majority also made some effort to insure literacy before the child could be put to work.

The Bureau understood that school would not replace work for children if their family's poverty were to be ignored. Hence, the Bureau crusaded for mothers' pensions (also called widows' pensions) and for laws to allow the government to search for errant husbands who had abandoned their families and make them pay support. The first statewide mandatory mothers' pension law was passed in Illinois in 1911. By 1920, forty-four jurisdictions had made desertion and abandonment a crime, while forty-three had also declared non-support illegal. By 1923, forty states had adopted this program. The need for a court to handle the distribution of mothers' pension moneys or to resolve charges of nonsupport led to the use of juvenile court for distribution of mothers' pensions, and, in some cases, the creation of family courts to hear charges of desertion.

Thanks to the Children's Bureau, progressives in the field of education, and the overall prosperity in the years prior to World War I, school attendance increased. By 1914, 19% of Americans of school age were enrolled in elementary school. School was limited, however. The average child attended for approximately 87 days out of a 159-day year. The typical school was a one-room schoolhouse with inadequately prepared teachers. In spite of the limitations, this was a sign that the *idea* of compulsory public school education was now being accepted by immigrant communities. High school enrollment showed the greatest gains, doubling in the years between 1898 and 1914, in part because working class families were attracted to the new commercial courses the high schools offered.

The National Child Labor Committee found that states regulated children's labor with varying degrees of compliance and scarcely at all in the South. The Committee filed legislation in Congress in 1916 to bring the federal government into the field. This bill, the Keatings-Owen Act, prohibited the interstate transportation of articles produced in factories or mines employing children under fourteen years of age (sixteen in the mines), or which employed children between fourteen and sixteen for more than eight hours a day, or at night. The bill passed both houses of Congress in September 1916 and was signed into law by a somewhat less than enthusiastic President Woodrow Wilson.

But supporters of federal legislation failed to reckon with the conservatism of the judiciary and the hostility of the South. The Southern Cotton Manufacturers Association prepared a case to challenge the new federal law.

Three days before the law was to go into effect, a federal district judge in North Carolina issued an injunction staying its enforcement in order to protect the rights of Reuben and John Dagenhart, aged fourteen and twelve respectively, to work more than eight hours a day. No previous decision had questioned Congress' power to bar objectionable commodities from interstate shipment. The Supreme Court had previously upheld congressional use of the commerce clause to exclude impure food, lottery tickets, liquor destined for dry states, and prostitutes (the white slave trade). Nevertheless, in *Hammer v. Dagenhart,* Justice William R. Day, writing for a five to four majority, found that the child-labor law was an improper exercise of Congress' power to regulate commerce.

After the decision in *Hammer v. Dagenhart,* Congress tried to repair the damage by using the Revenue Act of 1919 as a vehicle for heavily taxing goods produced by child labor. Congress had used discriminatory taxes before, with judicial approval, to discourage the production of other commodities which for one reason or another congressmen viewed as undesirable. It did this for such products as phosphorous matches, narcotics, and yellow oleomargarine. The fate that befell the first law soon overtook the second. Although it had previously sanctioned the application of prohibitory taxes, its attitude now appeared to be "that some limitation must be placed on the taxing device lest Congress gain unlimited power to regulate." Apparently, child labor was the right place to draw the line.

By the time the Court ruled in this case, the Progressive impulse had dissipated; child labor legislation would have to wait for another time.

The First Juvenile Court

Before the nineteenth century, the legal relationship between parent and child was largely based on English common law. The child actually had no rights as a *person.* If the child was heir to property, the law took strong notice and made sure a guardian was appointed to safeguard the *property*. The father's almost absolute power was granted in return for the efficient performance of parental duties. Those duties were defined as maintaining and protecting the child and providing suitable education. As the nineteenth-century moved forward American law modified paternal absolutism. This started when a few courts broke with centuries of precedent and decided custodial contests for children in favor of their mother rather than their father. These decisions introduced a concept new to Anglo-American jurisprudence, that is, a recognition of the child's welfare as a direct object of court interest. The courts gave their sanction to a child's *right* to security and safety, a right which could, under carefully defined circumstances, *override* the parents' natural right to the custody of their children.

But no body of law called "children's rights" had evolved from these few judicial assaults on parental authority. Rather, the growing belief that society, in some ill-defined way, owed children protection, grew from the teachings of the reformers of the Progressive Era. The juvenile court was one of the most promising creations to come out of this era.

The history of the juvenile court begins in Denver and Chicago. At the turn of the century, children aged fourteen or older, brought before the court on a "criminal matter," would be found guilty or innocent using exactly the same standards used for indicted adults. Children aged seven and under could never be guilty of a crime because they were legally incapable of forming necessary intent. Children between seven and fourteen were presumed incapable of criminal intent, but the presumption was "rebuttable." That is, the state could attempt to show that the child was mature beyond his years and should be held responsible. If the state succeeded in rebutting the presumption, the child would be tried as an adult. Children were also tried in the same courts as adults, although Boston pioneered the hearing of juveniles in altogether separate courtrooms in 1869.

The treatment of children after the conviction of crime was as harsh as the legal principles by which they were tried. Until the nineteenth century, juvenile offenders went to the same jails as adults and were even mutilated or executed in exactly the same manner as adults.

Denver, Colorado, in 1901 was an unlikely locale for a startling innovation in juvenile law. It was a "rough and ready" frontier town with a national reputation for its gambling halls, saloons, brothels, and harsh justice. In 1900, the state of Colorado regarded a ten year-old child old enough to try and punish under criminal law and, accordingly, had sent hundreds of youths to prison each year. This changed on a cold winter afternoon in 1901, when Judge Benjamin Barr Lindsey of the Denver County Court was presiding over a case dealing with a claim on some furniture in a warehouse. An assistant to the district attorney came up to the bench and asked the judge to interrupt his proceedings to hear a larceny case that would not take long. Lindsey agreed. The attorney returned with a little boy accused of stealing a piece of coal from the railroad tracks. Judge Lindsay found him guilty and sentenced him to State Reform School. James M. Hawes, quoting from Lindsey's autobiography *Children in Urban Society*, records what happened next: the Judge "was greeted with the most soul-piercing scream of agony that I ever heard." It was the boy's mother, who had just understood that she would lose her boy. Lindsey and the district attorney agreed to suspend his sentence. Lindsey conducted his own investigation. He went to the boy's unheated home and found that the father was ill with lead poisoning. Lindsey was profoundly distressed by the boy's situation; moreover, he knew this child's life was like countless others. Lindsey knew he could not change the economic circumstances of the boy's life. But he felt that he could change the *legal* circumstances.

Judge Lindsey wanted to create a separate court for children accused of criminal behavior. He proposed a "civil proceeding in equity." This legal concept was even older than English common law. It was the king's law. In the king's own court (also called the Court of Chancery), the individual stories of the defendant and plaintiff comprised the evidence. Lindsey wanted this kind of flexibility, where a child's real situation and character could be part of the courtroom proceedings. It allowed the judge to hear cases, fashion an appropriate punishment, and let the child go without establishing a criminal record. His court in Denver County became the nation's first municipal juvenile court. Lindsay continued his role of judge/social worker/substitute father till the day he died. He conducted a non-stop campaign to bring his ideas to courtrooms all over the country. His ideas were received with some enthusiasm, but at first, only one state, Illinois went so far as to create a statewide juvenile court. The comprehensive Illinois statute dealt with jurisdiction over and treatment of dependent and neglected, as well as delinquent, children. It was a radical step towards officially acknowledging that whatever the immediate act or situation, each case required understanding, guidance, and protection rather than concepts of criminal responsibility, guilt, and punishment. As nearly as possible, contentious criminal proceedings were eliminated. The legislation included an informal hearing instead of a formal trial, specially designated (though not necessarily specially qualified) judges, a special juvenile courtroom, and a separate "juvenile record." In addition, probation officers would be charged with the responsibility of conducting investigations, representing the interests of the child, taking custody over the child, and supervising it when necessary, whether the child was at home or in an institution.

The Boston Juvenile Court dates its origins to the year 1906, when it adopted a law that somewhat mirrored the Illinois statute. Boston practice differed slightly in two ways: it encouraged a parent to be present with the child in court, and it gave a large role to the investigating probation officer, continuing a successful practice it had begun as early as the 1870s.

By 1925, there were only two states in the nation (Maine and Wyoming) without legislatively created juvenile courts. The creation of these special courts was a step toward acknowledging that a juvenile delinquent was not simply a miniature adult who had chosen to break the law. Now he could be perceived as a child, immature and in need of help more than anything else. The juvenile courts gave judges options they would not have had otherwise. Judge Lindsey, for example, ran his own home for wayward boys. Also, the juvenile courts became the first courts to introduce mental-health information as part of the decision-making process. At the Boston Juvenile Court, Judge Harry Humphrey Baker, pioneered this work; today the "Judge Baker Clinic" stands as one of the best child-guidance clinics in the country.

Fortuitously, the early growth of the juvenile court movement paralleled the introduction into American life of Dr. Sigmund Freud's theories about the nature, behavior, and rights of children. The child-protection movement could now add a new right to the list of children's rights, the right to a healthy emotional life. This was added to the rights to be free of abuse and to be educated. The new "science" of psychiatry, with its compelling vocabulary, lent an authoritative voice to those who wished to erase for all time the theory that children were born evil, and substituted understanding of child development as a guide to the treatment of children.

Alas, the matching of juvenile court needs to psychology insights did not produce its hoped-for success. Juvenile court judges did not know how to use the new discipline's offerings, and the new discipline was itself limited in what it could provide. The hopes of the brave new world crashed on the shoals of humankind's inability to change. Developments at the Boston Juvenile Court will illustrate this unfortunate reality.

The Massachusetts legislature gave the new Boston Juvenile Court the task of administering mothers' pensions. This method of administering the pensions fell prey to the same abuse of class bias that all the other systems had. After an investigation by the court officer, the court might determine that the mother was unworthy of aid and remove the child from her home. Other juvenile courts adopted similar legislation. Placing children outside the home actually *increased* in the years 1900–1930. This expansion of foster care is attributed to the growth of the juvenile courts. Parents, now subject to an arm of the law and not simply a critical Friendly Visitor, were actually in a worse position for asserting their rights than they had been in the nineteenth century. The power of a juvenile judge was, for all practical purposes, unlimited. Some lawyers were critical of this power, claiming that parents had lost their due process rights. Lawyers were also critical of the suspension of rules of evidence at hearings for juvenile defendants. (This was the "informal setting" that had seemed a promising way to soften the harshness of court). They feared that what would work well in the hands of a caring judge could be abused by a judge who wanted simply to punish. They feared that the judgment of the law would be, as before, distorted by the class difference between the judge and the judged. Unfortunately, their fears came true all too quickly. In the decades that followed, the suspension of due process became just what juvenile court antagonists feared: an anomalous situation producing more punishment without any means of appeal.

When the juvenile court first appeared, its backers hailed it as a great innovation in the treatment of troubled children. When it failed to solve all of life's problems, criticism mounted. An editorial in a New York paper reminded its readers that "…after all, it is still a corrective agency of the state, dealing with the results of conditions that should as far as possible be prevented."

The editorial was correct as far as it went. It would have been more useful if it had informed the citizens as to how to prevent those "conditions."

CHAPTER FIVE

THE NEW DEAL
and WORLD WAR II

1933–1945

CHAPTER FIVE

The New Deal and World War II

1933–1945

Introduction

The Great Depression of 1929 was preceded by nearly a decade of economic prosperity that was marked by extravagance and flamboyance. Speculation and fraud in stock investments were widespread and, in the Midas-touch atmosphere, even admired. The new emphasis on consumer goods and the ready availability of purchase credit lent a sense of mastery over one's world, convincing too many that there was no limit to the quest for an ever-higher standard of living.[3]

The nation was rudely awakened by the stock market crash of October 24, 1929, the near collapse of the whole credit structure of the American economy, the spiral of falling sales, rising unemployment, declining income, and production cuts. Americans had profoundly believed that the nation would soon triumph over poverty. That belief now lay in tatters. Historian Richard Hofstadter wrote in *The Age of Reform*,

---

[3] In the summer of 1929, John J. Raskob, the millionaire chairman of the Democratic National Committee, said: "If a man saves $15.00 a week, and invests in good common stock, and allows the dividends and rights to accumulate, at the end of twenty years he will have at least $80,000 and an income of investments of around $400 a month. He will be rich. And because income can do that, I am firm in my belief that anyone cannot only be rich, but ought to be rich."

The Great Depression, which broke the mood of the twenties almost as suddenly as the postwar reaction had killed Progressive fervor, rendered obsolete most of the antagonisms that had flavored the politics of the postwar era. Once again, the demand for reform became irresistible, and out of the chaotic and often mutually contradictory schemes for salvation that arose from all corners of the country the New Deal took form. In the years 1933–1938 the New Deal sponsored a series of legislative changes that made the enactments of the Progressive Era seem timid by comparison.

The stock market crash in October and the long depression that followed shattered some long-cherished myths: that anyone who really wanted to work could find a job, that the middle class would be protected in a downturn, that the economic security of the rich would never be threatened.

The signs of depression set in rapidly: factories lay idle and stores had few customers. By 1933, the gross national product had fallen to half of what it had been in 1929. By 1933, the unemployment figure rose to 25% of the population, up from 4% in 1929. Hundreds of thousands of farmers were thrown off their land.

Historically, the outstanding fact about the New Deal was that it initiated a sharp turn in the history of American reformism, an abrupt break in the continuity with the past. By March 1933, when Franklin Delano Roosevelt took his oath of office, the entire working apparatus of American economic life had been smashed. With this smash-up went all support for a remote, silent federal government. The federal government was now expected to be responsible for nationwide regulation and the three Roosevelt R's: *Relief, Recovery, and Reform.*

With this smash-up went the hundred-and-fifty-year sacred alliance of the Supreme Court and the barons of capitalism. During President Roosevelt's *first* term the Court invalidated no less than twelve pieces of legislation passed by Congress to relieve the economic distress of the country. In his second term, however, New Deal legislation was validated in a series of decisions that put the Supreme Court squarely behind the president's program of recovery and reform.

PART ONE

Government Programs

Franklin Delano Roosevelt became president on March 4, 1933, and immediately set to work on the most urgent problem, *relief.* In so doing, he set in motion a revolution in American history; henceforth, all questions about federal and state government involvement in social and economic programs would be about the *degree* of involvement; questions about the *correctness* of involvement would never again be asked.

The most direct relief effort of the federal government was the Federal Emergency Relief Act (FERA). Congress appropriated $500 million and FDR gave the funds to FERA administrator, Harry Hopkins, to disburse to the states. Within one month—working from a desk in the hallway because his office was not yet ready—he paid out his first fifty-one million dollars. Eventually, four billion was expended in a program that touched twenty million people. It is important to note that this was a *needs-based* program. One of FERA's most far-reaching effects was the requirement that relief monies be distributed only through public, not private, agencies. This ended the participation of voluntary/private agencies in poor relief, closing a chapter in the history of American charity.

The largest welfare program of the New Deal, and of American history, began on January 15, 1935, when the Committee on Economic Security submitted its report to the president and he in turn transmitted it to Congress. The Social Security Act (SSA), which emerged several months later, became law on August 14, 1935. It had passed with only six dissenting votes in the Senate and thirty-three dissenting votes in the House.

The SSA was another landmark in American political and social history, reflecting a governmental shift from a concern for property rights to a concern for the rights of people, and, consequently, extending federal responsibility for social welfare.

The Social Security Act was an omnibus measure financed through the taxing powers of the federal government (a device already held by the Supreme Court to be constitutional). It established two lines of attack against destitution, social insurance and public assistance. The social insurance program consisted of (1) a pension program guaranteed to all people (and their spouses) who had been part of the work force when they turned sixty-five, and (2) unemployment insurance. Pensions were for all retirees across the nation; no means test was applied. The program is currently administered by the Social Security Administration of the Department of Health and Human Services.

The social revolution it wrought was profound, for it affected three generations simultaneously. Until the date of its passage, children typically supported aged parents. The financial burden on the average wage earner was considerable, forcing him to choose between his parents' needs and his children's. This act, then, also contributed to the financial well-being of children.

The second of the two social insurance programs was unemployment insurance (or compensation) for the temporarily jobless. Unlike old-age pensions, this program is jointly administered by the federal and state governments.: it is financed by taxes collected by the U.S. Department of the Treasury, but administered by the states.

The public assistance provisions of the New Deal fell into the following defined categories: old age insurance for those not eligible for work-related pensions, the blind, the disabled, and, in a separate category, Aid to Dependent Children (ADC).

Aid to Dependent Children was the most controversial program of the Social Security Act. Originally, the Children's Bureau was expected to administer it and to provide for all needy children, including those in intact families. A distaste for the "pro-child" perspective of the Children's Bureau led Congress to shift administration to the Labor Department and, in the final bill, aid was restricted to families where the father had died or deserted the family. The amount of money appropriated per child was one half the amount appropriated for each old age pensioner. A review of this thin offering for children suggests that there was no person or agency available to argue on behalf of children's needs specifically.

However, children were significantly helped by the Maternal and Child Welfare Act, part of the SSA. Instead of providing cash payment to persons in need, it funded specific programs. Some of the numerous programs it funded were: child-welfare services for the care of homeless, dependent, and neglected children, and those in danger of becoming delinquent; vocational training and rehabilitation for crippled and physically handicapped children; and the promotion of the health of children and mothers. The latter included prenatal and birthing care for mothers. The federal government and the states share funding for these programs. Administration is by state agency. The use of a state agency to administer ADC ended the always-dubious role of the juvenile courts in administering mothers' pensions. It paved the way for separate child-welfare agencies to emerge as the dominant child-welfare model.

Since the administration was unable to get a national health insurance bill through Congress (the American Medical Association lobbied vigorously against it), left wing critics were highly critical of the Social Security Act. They pointed to many additional failures of the bill: it provided no long-term disability insurance; only "regular" workers were covered; there was no coverage for farm laborers, domestic servants, or workers' dependents.

Its flaws notwithstanding, one must look at what Social Security did accomplish to see why it is regarded as a landmark in American history. What did it do? It nationalized and improved welfare services. It led to the creation of public welfare departments in almost every American county. It acknowledged beyond dispute that external forces begat personal poverty, not individual weakness. Poverty (at least temporarily) was de-stigmatized.

The Social Security Act also established a new alignment of responsibility in the field of public welfare. It marked the beginning of a policy of federal aid to the states, closing the door at long last on three centuries of the Elizabethan poor law with its emphasis on *local* responsibility. In subsequent years, the seed planted by SSA sprouted into wider coverage and more benefits.

Some social historians think it has helped more people escape from poverty than all other federal programs combined.[4]

---

[4] Historical note: It had been almost 100 years (1854) since President Franklin Pierce vetoed a bill to assist the indigent insane, explaining to Dorothea Dix, a 19th c. crusader for humane treatment of the mentally ill, that the life conditions of individuals were no proper concern of the federal government.

PART TWO

Children and Youth

Children as a class were severely harmed by the Depression. Infant death rates and early childhood malnutrition rose sharply. This was especially true in the rural areas where the loss of the extension of the Shephard-Towner clinics doomed any hope of getting health care to the rural poor. Estimates of homeless children at the time run as high as 1.25 million. The census bureau in 1931 reported that 200,000 people under the age of twenty-one were homeless and rootless, roaming the land. The states where they temporarily deposited themselves refused them assistance. FERA took up the slack, giving money to the states to provide camps and shelters for transients; in 1935 it assisted 40,000 transient families and 118,00 singles, including 30,000 boys and 350 girls under the age of twenty-one. Juvenile crime in urban areas increased dramatically. "Hungry children have a tendency to steal food," stated a sage social worker to a juvenile court judge.

Work

Where the law allowed children to work, the Depression offered them two contradictory alternatives. On one hand they could be more easily exploited. Until the passage of the Fair Labor Standards Act (1938), they could be required to work long hours for a pittance, of which their families needed every cent. But a more positive experience was available to some older children—getting a job with a New Deal agency, learning a trade, and being paid an adult's wage. Compared to the "Roaring Twenties," which produced a significant generational divide for the first time in American History, the Depression brought the generations together, as family members pulled together to put food on the table and keep a roof over their heads.

But the Roosevelt administration wished to enable as many adults as possible to obtain work; in this regard it did not want youth to compete for the agency jobs. It developed two programs specifically targeted to youth. The first was the National Youth Administration (NYA) which offered four programs for youth aged sixteen to twenty-five: work-study for students for families on relief, vocational assistance, and organized recreation. Over two and one half million young people were involved in work projects during the NYA years (1935–1943). The NYA was supposed to train equal numbers of male and female youths in equally marketable skills. The training of women became serious, however, only as World War II approached and the draft depleted the ranks of young men. Despite some obvious biases, the NYA dealt more directly with the issue of race than many other New Deal agencies, in part thanks to black activist Mary Mcleod Bethune. As a member of the NYA advisory committee and the National Association for the Advancement of Colored People, Bethune worked to make sure that young Negro Americans received equal services through the NYA. Fortunately, she had sufficient stature to command the right audience and she achieved modest success in an area where many others had tried and failed. America's entry into World War II eliminated the need for the National Youth Administration, and it closed its doors in 1943. From its inception it had aided over 600,000 college-aged youth and over one and one-half million high-school-aged youth.

The most imaginative of the programs for youth was the Civilian Conservation Corps (CCC). This organization was a favorite of the president's because it promoted two of his interests simultaneously: the preservation of natural resources and the development of human resources. The CCC received a grant of $300 million to enroll young men aged eighteen to twenty-five from relief families to work on reforestation, soil conservation, and flood control.

They were given room and board and $30 a month, of which $25 was sent to their families. More than 2.75 million boys from across the country were placed in rural locations they had never before heard of, making contributions of lasting value (for example, planting tree lines on the Great Plains to break sandstorms). The blot on the CCC record, no surprise, has to do with its policy on race. Bowing to the habitual Southern opposition to anything that potentially assisted the black population, the CCC adopted a racial quota, allowing no more than 3% of the total enrollment to be black. Even when black participation was enlarged, segregation in training classes and job placement remained the rule.

The last major New Deal reform measure affecting children was the Fair Labor Standards Act of June 1938. This act was critical for industrial workers and for children, although it did not cover farm labor because Southern Democrats opposed coverage for farm workers. The Fair Labor Standards Act established age sixteen as the minimum for child employees, essentially abolishing child labor. Businessmen faced fines if underage youths were found on their payrolls. The act established a maximum workweek of forty hours for all industrial workers and a minimum wage of twenty-five cents an hour, to be raised to forty cents after eight years. Americans were shocked to learn that 750,000 laborers received a wage *increase* on the day the law went into effect on August 1, 1938.

The Fair Labor Standards Act passed constitutional muster. Thirty-three years after *Hammer v. Dagenhart* (the North Carolina case which prohibited Congress from legislating minimum wages or length of work day for children), the Supreme Court overruled its own precedent. Justice Harlan F. Stone, writing for a unanimous Court in *U.S. v. Darby* (1941) ruled that once goods were placed in the stream of interstate commerce, the federal government could legislate anything it chose that involved the manufacture of the goods.

Education

An interesting sidelight to youth unemployment was the growth of high school attendance. One hundred and twelve years after Boston opened the first public high school in the United States, the majority of American youth were now enrolled in high school. What began as "something to do if we can't work" became so popular that expectations changed. By 1940, an overwhelming majority of young people were enrolled, and an expectation developed that everyone would attend high school, and perhaps even graduate. High school was made more appealing to the working class by changing the high-school curriculum. Formerly, college preparatory courses (Greek and Latin) dominated the curriculum; now one could also study business subjects to prepare for work in the everyday world.

Day Care

The federal government, through the federal Emergency Relief Administration, provided funding for day-care centers for working parents. These centers freed women to work *and* provided jobs for unemployed teachers, nurses, nutritionists, clerical workers, cooks, and janitors. By 1937 the FERA money that employed WPA workers also set up 1,900 day care centers for about 40,000 children. It was a very popular program.

The initial level of funding became inadequate to the need once the war broke out. Although interagency squabbling had slowed it down, by July 1943 the government was committing huge amounts of money to childcare centers so moms could work in war production factories.

The building and staffing of the centers began slowly. But the war produced an insatiable need for materiel and workers. Young men were drafted; young women were ready, willing, and able, but they had children. Only group childcare would make the women available. Despite this, opposition to out-of-home childcare in the Senate remained strong. The women's auxiliary of certain industrial unions, community leaders, FWA officials, and the six women of the House of Representatives joined in order to lobby Congress to keep federal funds rolling. By emphasizing the need to maintain wartime production goals, they were able to obtain more funds. But the victory was ephemeral and did not survive past the war; as soon as it was over, Congress cut the funding.

The need for childcare during the war became the source of truly innovative private business experiments. An outstanding example is the day care that Edgar F. Kaiser organized in his two enormous shipyards in Vanport City, Oregon. To house workers and their families, the government erected its largest wartime civilian housing project, called Vanport City, Oregon. Foreseeing that 25,000 female workers would need childcare, Kaiser constructed two large child-care centers, naming the head of the Institute of Child Development at Columbia University as the director. He located the buildings at the entrance to the shipyards, making them convenient for mothers on their way to and from work. Kaiser provided grassy play areas, four wading pools, fifteen classrooms, an infirmary with a trained nurse, a social worker, and a fully-staffed kitchen. The funding for this glorious enterprise came from Kaiser, the federal government, and nominal fees charged to the mothers themselves.

Another option for wartime childcare was an unheralded but unique program called Extended School Services (ESS), an extended school-age day care.

It was one of the biggest success stories of the war. Working mothers of school-age children vastly outnumbered working mothers of preschoolers; the needs of these mothers and their young children were acute. In August 1942, President Roosevelt allocated $400,000 to the U.S. Office of Education and the Children's Bureau for the promotion of and coordination of programs for the school-age children of working mothers. The money was to be distributed by various state agencies. The initial response from the states was lukewarm. However, by mid-1943 local communities in thirty-three states had established ESS programs. Even when federal funds were terminated, a combination of state, local, and private funds kept the programs going throughout the war. This changed, however, after the war, when the entire country, women included, thought that nothing was more important than getting women out of the workplace and back in the home, raising children. It would be twenty years before the call for day care was heard again.

PART THREE

Family Courts, Juvenile Probation

The rapid move of state legislatures toward the creation of juvenile courts failed to improve the position of the juvenile (or his family) in court. This was due, again, to the expanded role of the juvenile court judge.

He was redefined as the person who acted in the child's *best interest.* That is, he was asked to act as though he were the director of a social service agency. This happened by accident. In the early twentieth century, the development of children's services was in its infancy. There was no other agency that could be charged with such a broad responsibility, so it made sense to encourage the juvenile court to become the repository of all administrative functions affecting children. Thus, as in Massachusetts, the judge in the juvenile court became the administrator of Mother's Aid, the finder of foster homes, the counselor for unwed mothers, and the enforcer of school attendance laws. The hybrid nature of the courts, law enforcers, and social agencies confused the public. In the minds of some citizens, the juvenile court would not only adjudicate juvenile delinquency cases, it would *prevent* them from happening.

Inevitably, in line with the criticism previously leveled at the role of the juvenile court judges this extensive use of the juvenile court invited criticism. Due process rights of parents seemed to have vanished. Although the parents' interest was recognized everywhere and a child could not be taken from his parents' home and institutionalized without some opportunity to contest the proceeding, these protections were more theoretical than actual. A number of realities worked to nullify parents' rights. Between 1907 and 1911, over 90% of the children brought into the juvenile courts were the offspring of European immigrants. Their parents did not speak English. The only legal counsel available charged fees (no Legal Services Corporation), and parents did not have the funds to pay. The legal game was that the court knew that the parent had violated his duty to his child; it was the burden of the parent to prove otherwise. When, predictably, the parent could not, the court was free to send the child to an institution of its choosing. To this writer's knowledge, no appeal was ever made. Attorney Douglas R. Rendleman, writing in the South Carolina Law Review, says that from the very beginning the role of the equity court and the doctrine of *parens patriae* (the court as parent) was purposely misunderstood and misapplied. The absence of standard civil procedure rules redounded to the harm of the parents, not their benefit. "The statutes exacerbated the vulnerability of a class of people; and because of the porous and opaque definitions and the flimsy procedures, the state was allowed to interpose pretty much its own will."

The creation of the juvenile court was to be accompanied by two additional reforms. The first was that youth who were detained and then, if necessary, jailed, were to be housed in facilities separate from adult defenders. The second was that the young person must be treated as an individual, that the judge and his probation officers must have personal knowledge about the offender. This personal knowledge was important; it was to be used to fashion an appropriate placement. In both instances, the reforms foundered.

Two major problems emerged. In most jurisdictions the juvenile courts were inadequately financed. For example, the original Illinois Juvenile Court Act authorized appointment of a probation staff, but did not authorize money to pay them. The all-important plan of establishing separate detention facilities *never happened* in Cook County because the state legislature withheld funds. In fact, in spite of the specific provisions to the contrary, children continued to be imprisoned with adult criminals in county and city jails. If this happened in Illinois, the first and most supportive region of statewide juvenile courts, one can imagine the situation in the rest of the nation.

A related issue involved the caliber of court personnel. To a considerable extent, this issue was a reflection of budgetary limitations, but it had another side. At some point in the early history of the juvenile court, enthusiasm for it waned. It may simply have been a common occurrence experienced by other movements: when the inspired founders leave a movement, those who never really shared the vision replace them. For whatever reasons, good judges began to decline appointments to the juvenile bench and inferior judges were appointed in their place. Since this was a court which demanded committed, energetic, intelligent judges to make it succeed, it began to fail. For this reason the juvenile courts failed to be leaders on behalf of underprivileged children, failed to educate the community about the lives of these children, and failed the children who became, once again, a mass without an individual face.

More than any other group, probation officers provided the juvenile court with some humanity. The National Probation Association published articles in its annual yearbook that alerted its membership, and the casual reader, to problems that were developing in the juvenile courts. It was one of the first organizations that worked with children who were either neglected or delinquent to point out that the child brought into court under a petition for neglect or abuse was often the same child brought to court on delinquency charges (1935–1936 Yearbook of the National Probation Association). It examined the problems of a juvenile court that heard delinquency cases *and* care-and-protection cases with the same set of rules. How, they asked, was a court accustomed to finding either criminal guilt or innocence going to accustom itself to the nuances of child protection cases?

Probation officers strove to bring the matter of *classification* to the attention of the lawmakers. *Classification* was a shorthand way of describing the labeling of the juvenile and his crime. The category of crime determined the harshness of the juvenile's sentence, always called the "disposition" of the case. Reformers charged that greater attention had to be paid to classification, because without it, juveniles charged with minor crimes would be treated exactly the way serious adult offenders were treated.

The Massachusetts legislature finally took the classification problem seriously. In 1939, it appointed a special commission to study the problem of classification and to make recommendations, commenting, "The greatest criticism which can be made of the procedure in this Commonwealth in the treatment of juvenile delinquents is inadequate and improper classification." As if these were new concepts, the Commission recommended the creation of a Classification Board, before whom individuals could be presented for individual recommendations of disposition. It urged that a system of juvenile courts be established separate and apart from any other courts, one "skilled in the treatment of juvenile problems." This was twenty-eight years after the enactment of a juvenile court law that had very similar language. In time, reformers would learn whether or not Massachusetts youth would benefit from this report.

CHAPTER SIX

THE TRUMAN-EISENHOWER ERA ECONOMIC PROSPERITY, SOCIAL TURMOIL

1945–1960

CHAPTER SIX

The Truman-Eisenhower Era Economic Prosperity, Eddies of Social Turmoil

1945–1960

Introduction

On April 12, 1945, President Franklin Delano Roosevelt died and an era ended. Harry S. Truman, willing, able, but untried and unknown, inherited the office of the presidency. He was determined to pursue the social welfare goals of the New Deal. On September 6, 1945, three weeks after V-J Day, Truman sent a twenty-one-point program on domestic legislation to Congress. The program included proposals ensuring full employment for public housing, farm price supports, the nationalization of atomic energy, health insurance, a permanent Fair Employment Practices Commission, and an updating of New Deal legislation on conservation, social security, and minimum wage. A Congress dominated by Republicans who were deeply desirous of reversing the New Deal temporarily blocked this agenda. After he won the 1948 election, however, Truman was able to enact his agenda. In time, this legislation would be described as "The Fair Deal."

The Truman Era was marked at first by high inflation. However, as soon as the troops were home and settled into their new three-bedroom houses, consumption and prosperity ruled the day.

Black Americans experienced far less heart-warming circumstances. Despite their efforts during wartime, there was still vicious hostility among the general American public any time their civil rights were discussed. Blacks began to use the courts to redress their grievances. The triumph of this era was the victory of Thurgood Marshall, chief counsel for the National Association for the Advancement of Colored People, before the Supreme Court. In a case titled *Brown v. Board of Education*, he won a 9-0 decision that overturned a fifty-eight-year ruling that had made segregation in public facilities and public schools legal.

Chief Justice Warren, speaking for a unanimous Court, said that in the field of education, the concept of "separate but equal" was a constitutional nullity—separate educational facilities were inherently unequal. "To separate (black children) from others of similar age and qualifications solely because of their race generates a feeling of inferiority as to their status in the community that may affect their hearts and minds in a way never to be undone. *Plessy v. Ferguson* (1896)[5] was explicitly overruled. With one stroke the Court undercut the entire structure of the Jim Crow laws.

For each of the three succeeding Septembers, the opening day of school was marked by violence in the South. In September 1957, President Eisenhower had to use federal troops to protect the nine black children trying to enter

---

[5] In *Plessy v. Ferguson* a Negro citizen sued for the right to sit where he chose on a streetcar for which he had paid full fare. The Supreme Court ruled that separate accommodations did not deprive Negroes of the equal protection of the law if the accommodations afforded Negroes were equal to those afforded whites. The doctrine of "separate but equal" rapidly became the standard for public accommodations and public school.

school in Little Rock, Arkansas. The remainder of the student body, and all teachers but one (an Army wife newly arrived from the North) boycotted the school. The threat of violence hung thick in the air.

Organized black protest gained inspiration from these confrontations of students and the power structure. In 1955, the Reverend Martin Luther King Jr. led a successful bus boycott in Montgomery, Alabama, forcing the city fathers to operate buses in which any seat on any bus was available to any person who paid the fare. And on February 1, 1960, in Greensboro, North Carolina, four black freshmen from the Negro Agricultural and Technological College sat down at a whites-only lunch counter at Woolworth's Department Store. The sit-in movement was born. As the Eisenhower presidency was drawing to a close, race relations in America was shifting gears.

PART ONE

Prosperity, modified

In 1956, almost without notice, the United States hurried by a milestone comparable in significance to the disappearance of the American frontier in the 1890s. The government issued figures indicating that the number employed in the worker's job of producing things was now less than the number making their livings from largely middle-class occupations. More than half the population had reached or was just about to reach white-collar status.

Eric F. Goldman, *The Crucial Decade*

The expansion of the middle class and the comfort of the nation as it increasingly defined itself as a "middle-class country" describe this phase of American history. The years from 1940 to 1960 are marked by a transition from the search for money to buy goods to a search for goods on which to spend money. Between 1940 and 1970, the gross national product, taking inflation into account, tripled. Real disposable income more than doubled. Family income, and therefore family welfare measured in monetary terms, showed significant improvement. Most income groups of the population shared in the prosperity, although, as will be seen one-quarter of the population did not. Since Dwight David Eisenhower had been elected to the presidency in 1952, the ten year period of the fifties is informally called called "Eisenhower prosperity."

Non-white family income did move up, but not as rapidly as white family income. The gap between incomes, even in this prosperous time, widened. The consequences of racial discrimination in hiring were that the lowest segment of the economy did not participate in "Eisenhower prosperity." In 1960, almost 40 million people, or 22.4 % of the population, lived below the poverty line of

$3,022 a year for a family of four.[6] This frustration of black aspirations, coming at a time when they believed they would finally be able to participate in the economic mainstream, fueled the growing rights-protest movement.

The availability of more and better skilled labor and more and better technology fed prosperity for the white majority. The labor force maintained its wartime expansion, and there were now civilian jobs for workers to make the products the postwar prosperity demanded. The number of women in the work force grew from 24% during the war to more than 43% in 1960. The absolute number of Americans grew as birth rates steadily rose from 1945 to the mid-1960s, and the increase in life expectancy rose from 62.9 in 1940 to 69.7 in 1960.

The key to postwar affluence was increased output per man-hour. A steady development of new materials, new products, and new industries created new processes, specialized labor-saving machinery, and mass-production techniques. These new processes were enhanced by the development of computer technology, advanced information systems, and systems engineering. World War II had given a big boost to the chemical and airplane industries, and to the development and exploitation of synthetics such as nylon and metals such as aluminum. The transportation industry expanded with the growth of private ownership of automobiles for every American, and the growth of commercial aviation.

Government Programs

During the war, the government was mainly concerned with helping the families who had given up fathers, sons, and husbands to the national effort.

---

[6] The "poverty line," frequently used as a quick way of determining who is really poor, was developed early in the 1960s. It was the amount of the budget that constituted a short-term emergency diet times a factor of three, since it was estimated that a family should not have to spend more than one-third of its budget on food.

The Serviceman's Dependent Allowance Act of 1942, under the War Department, provided family allotments. After the war, the government legislated the Serviceman's Readjustment Act of 1944, called the G.I. (initials stood for "government issue") Bill of Rights. It provided stipends to support veterans and their families while the veterans went to school for vocational or higher education. They also paid for tuition, some home loans, business and farm loans, unemployment insurance payments, and veterans' employment services. The G.I. Bill contributed significantly to the improved quality of the post-war work force. Further, the government, attentive to the mental health needs of veterans, passed the National Mental Health Act of 1946, which funded research and training in mental health and established community mental-health services. An important by-product of these government-funded programs was that people with mental health problems no longer had to be locked away from public view.

The public warmly received a host of new government programs. In addition to the bills for "deserving veterans," the Truman and Eisenhower administrations joined with Congress to pass a host of other socially and economically useful measures. Between 1946 and 1960 Congress passed the National School Lunch Program and the Special Milk Program. Lawmakers created an Indian Health Service and an Employment Act that set a goal of maximum employment as a government policy. Congress expanded Old Age Survivors Insurance and added disability insurance to the social security program. This enabled families on welfare to obtain government aid when a member was seriously ill. In the year 1951, after unconscionable stalling, a meaningful anti-lynching law was put into place. Finally, the decade was rounded out with federal funding extended to child welfare services in rural areas, and, in 1960, the passage of the Kerr-Mills Act, providing aid to the medically indigent.

What the government could not achieve was universal health insurance. The need seemed obvious to all but the medical profession. As soon as he was inaugurated, President Eisenhower appointed the President's Commission on the Health Needs of the Nation. The Commission delivered its Report in 1953. Its findings were similar to those made in 1932 by the Committee on the Cost of Medical Care, in 1935 by the National Health Survey, and in 1948 by the National Health Congress. It called for a national system for reporting diseases, acknowledged that a significant number of Americans had no access to health care, and concluded that health care was too costly for the average American. The author of the report, Dean A. Clark, M.D., General Director of Massachusetts General Hospital in Boston, observed that the nation had the resources for a much larger preventive health program. Clark concluded the five-volume report by calling for a grant-in-aid program to states to encourage them to devise a plan of prepaid health insurance for a wide distribution of medical/health services. The well-organized American Medical Association blocked every proposal at every turn, and not one of these proposed measures passed.

Prosperity generates complacency. The ills of society are reflected through the lens of good times. White Americans in the second half of the 1950s settled into a complacent, consumer-oriented, conservative life, with their prosperity secure, foreign wars behind them, and the post-war agitation over the spread of communism all but forgotten. The prevailing attitude was that there were probably still some poor people somewhere, but the problem of poverty was rapidly disappearing in the affluent society.[7] Anyway, they would have concluded, we had a public welfare system to deal with those who were inexplicably absent from the nation's table.

---

[7] A phrase made popular when economist John Kenneth Galbraith published his description of America at mid-century, titled, *The Affluent Society*.

PART TWO

Children

The massive government effort to provide day care during World War II was abandoned when the war ended. It had been an expedient. The end of the war, the return of the troops, the change to a peacetime economy, and the return of men to jobs formerly held by women made day care, like rationing, seem an unhappy necessity during emergency. On February 28, 1946, when funds for day care and other social service programs were withdrawn, the federal government officially ended its support for childcare services. Several states and localities continued to operate them on a limited basis, providing public support to twelve thousand pre-school children—a fraction of the former numbers and a fraction of the need.

The closing of twenty-eight hundred centers left over a million and a half children without day-care services. Leaders and citizens alike assumed that working women would return to their rightful places at home to care for their children and fathers would return to their natural place in the workplace as breadwinners. Yet labor force statistics indicated that many women did not give up their jobs after the war. Studies show that between April 1948 and March 1966 the labor force participation of married women with husbands and with children under six increased from 11% to 24%. The *need* for day care continued, but support for it did not. Those who argued for expanded publicly-funded day care faced impossible odds. The curtain had rung down on public support for women working outside their homes. A combination of ideological, economic, and psychological reasons precluded serious consideration of the needs of working mothers and young children for day-care services.

In 1951, one of the most influential child-development books to reach this side of the Atlantic, a study of infant-maternal bonding, was written by the eminent English psychiatrist John Bowlby. Bowlby studied infants and children who had spent their childhood in England, separated from their parents during the war. Bowlby found a series of significant adjustment problems among these children. From these and other studies, he concluded that the underlying predictor of adult mental health is the infant's warm, intimate, and continuous relationship with his/her mother (or permanent mother substitute). Without this bonding, an infant's growth would become stunted physically, emotionally, and intellectually. Physically, the child would be less responsive to stimuli, and in cases of severe deprivation, the child would fail to thrive, and die. Emotionally, the child would remain immature, unable to resolve anger or develop trust, and be closed to human relationships.

Further research refined the Bowlby thesis, noting the distinction between separation and deprivation, probing the difference between temporary and permanent separation, and factoring in the role of extreme trauma (such as living through a war).

Modification of Bowlby's findings, however, did not weaken his central thesis; his work remained an important contribution to the understanding of maternal-infant bonding and its importance to the emotional wellbeing of an adult. Policy makers concluded that all legislation and policy should support the need of a mother to be with her young child. Certainly, it provided a persuasive argument for social workers striving to keep very young children from being placed in institutions.

In the wrong hands, regrettably, Bowlby's work gave credence to society's most potent message at that time: WOMEN, STAY HOME; YOUR CHILDREN NEED YOU. Every branch of the media reinforced this message. When social problems like the rise in juvenile delinquency exploded into the national consciousness of the 1950s, working mothers became the prime target.

The emotional needs of children, ignored in the nineteenth century, were now on everyone's agenda. Sigmund Freud's theories of emotional development, known in some minimal form by a surprising number of Americans, had set the stage. Now, from the White House Conference on Children and Youth to the halls of Harvard University, the central question was "What does a child need?"

For the first time in its history, the decennial White House Conference on Children and Youth focused on children's emotional needs. The 6,000 participants agreed to the Conference Report, which called for hospitals to get more involved in the mental health aspects of pregnancy, childbirth, and infant care, and for medical personnel and schools to coordinate their efforts to promote the physical and mental health of children.

Approaching child developmental needs from an entirely different point of view were a group of American psychologists who called themselves Behaviorists. Led by B. F. Skinner of Harvard University, the behaviorists focused on the step-by-step process by which a young child learns his or her tasks. They recommended that the child be carefully regulated, with little freedom to explore. This would make the child feel secure. Each correct move was to be rewarded, and each incorrect move was to be gently discouraged. This quick punishment or reward response, administered in small doses, was the best way to modify behavior. Aside from Skinner himself, who developed a box in which he could place his pre-ambulatory daughter so that he could carefully regulate her behavior, child raising does not seem to have been heavily impacted by the Behaviorists.

Sadly, this new interest in the well-being of children did little to arrest the growth of one of the more unsettling trends to emerge in the fifties, juvenile delinquency. For America's youth, especially in the large cities, this was a time without community and without structure. The war had left a legacy of geographical mobility. Serviceman and their families had scattered across the country. People seeking work had traveled to the locations of the new defense industries. New communities without roots grew up quickly. Migrants from rural areas, especially the South, created an urban population explosion. The youth, turning to each other for self-definition and community, became an urban threat.

The number of jobs available to a school dropout had declined steadily since the end of World War II. Although youth counselors who were paying attention to the large number of unemployed roaming the city streets described the situation as "social dynamite," they were speaking to an empty auditorium. By 1953, the number of youth termed delinquent was 45% higher than in 1948. By 1957, 23.5 out of every 1,000 children 10 to 17 years of age were in juvenile court on delinquency charge, double the 1948 rate. Now alerted, the nation responded quickly to society's needs to be protected from youthful behavior that challenged public authority. The FBI, seeing this exclusively as a matter of criminal law-breaking, sought to approach the problem in its usual "find-'em-and-lock-'em-up style." The Children's Bureau wanted to characterize the problem as "children-who-are-victims-of-circumstances-they-cannot-control." The battle had begun and, in one form or another, still continues today.

Congress briefly addressed a series of issues that the media sensationalized, such as the role of comic books in causing juvenile violence or the extreme dangers to which children working on farms were subjected. But nothing sustained their interest for very long. What did sustain their interest was government's payment to dependent children.

Early in the Eisenhower administration, Congress expanded Aid to Dependent Children (ADC), adding aid to a parent of a dependent child. Between 1953 and 1960, the families receiving ADC (now more commonly called AFDC—Aid to Families with Dependent Children) increased from 1,942,381 to 3,080,257. Within just a few years of its passage, AFDC was supporting far more children than institutions and foster care combined.

The swelling welfare rolls caught the attention of taxpayers. First in the South, but quickly spreading throughout the North, families were subjected to an "unsuitability test." States adopted regulations that denied support to children whose mothers had never married, were divorced, or were in common-law relationships with other men, thus denying support to a great many children. Using this test, Louisiana dropped 6,000 families from its welfare rolls. This "suitable home test" became an increasingly frequent device used to deny aid. Echoes of the past could be heard as the children of the poor were once again being punished for the behavior of their parents.

In the field of health care, America's children fared no better. In 1949, the funding for the wartime Emergency Maternity and Infant Care program ended. Congress refused to appropriate further funds for it. By the time the program ended in 1949, about one and a half million mothers and infants had received assistance. Although it improved child health, Congress made it clear that *its primary purpose was to improve the morale of American soldiers.* Just as it dismissed the need for day care, Congress refused to fund this "wartime measure." With the help of the Children's Bureau, the state of Washington tried to continue health care on an experimental basis. The American Academy of Pediatrics bitterly opposed it, stating that,"...the function of the Children's

Bureau has been abruptly changed so that it now is an active factor in the practice of medicine throughout the United States, dictatorially regulating fees and conditions of practice on a federal basis." (J. M. Hawes, quoting the *Journal of Pediatrics* in *The Children's Rights Movement*.) The opposition of the established medical organization *representing children* meant there would be no program and no support.

The astonishing fact is that, once again, the American Medical Association stood as the single force blocking the delivery of medical care to American citizens.

Juvenile Justice

The end of the Second World War heralded demands for redemption of the wartime promises of democracy and justice. The American judicial system, especially juvenile justice, came under renewed scrutiny and criticism. *Proponents* of juvenile courts were bitterly disappointed with the insignificant improvement in genuinely humane treatment for juvenile offenders. Angry *critics* of the juvenile courts were convinced that the juvenile court itself had contributed to the rise in delinquency by coddling delinquents.

The proponents reviewed the Standards for Juvenile Courts first adopted by the Children's Bureau in 1923 and codified by Congress in the Federal Juvenile Delinquency Act of 1938. The standards included adequate detention facilities separate from adults; broad jurisdiction for children under eighteen; judges chosen for their special qualifications for juvenile court work; informal court procedure; cases to be held promptly, privately, without a jury; a well-qualified probation staff for investigation; and resources for individual and specialized treatment.

Juvenile court observers could see that none of these provisions were in operation. They noted the repeated failure to build facilities that separated pre-trial detention of juveniles from adults, lack of investigation, flagrant abuse of due process rights, and indifferent, even hostile, judges. They concluded that, ironically, many juveniles would have been better protected if the standard adult procedures governed them in court.

Studies undertaken from 1918 to the 1950s revealed an all-too-familiar-fact: states refused to appropriate the money to build separate pre-trial facilities. In 1950, Albert Deutsch reported in *Our Neglected Children* that juveniles and adults were commonly warehoused together in pre-trial facilities that resembled "storage bins" (old jails, old almshouses). Juveniles were consistently subjected to physical abuse.

In 1948, the Massachusetts legislature, responding to reports of pre-trial abuses, passed legislation committing the care of all arrested juveniles to the probation department; this department was charged with providing safe-keeping of the juveniles in specialized foster homes or otherwise.

By 1952, the law's mandate still unfulfilled, the Massachusetts legislature tried again. It created the Division of Youth Services (DYS) as a sub-unit of the Department of Education. Detained youth that were not offered or could not meet bail were now placed in DYS facilities. This time it worked. Forty-six years after the passage of the Juvenile Court Act, Massachusetts achieved the goal of separating juvenile detainees from adults.

The second part of the standard, concerning investigations to assist in sentencing (disposition), would depend on the presence of a responsible probation department and, if available, a court clinic. According to the Children's Bureau study of 1918, only thirteen courts, all in large cities, maintained clinics for court cases. They were used more to collect data than help to determine disposition, their alleged purpose. Only with the onset of post-war "psychological thinking" did some of the big city courts get clinics that helped diagnose the juvenile and make limited recommendations about disposition.

Between 1900 and 1910, all the state legislatures but two adopted juvenile court legislation; probation officers in those years were volunteers and played the role of Friendly Visitors. They were not equipped to do the investigative work the court required. During the twenties, a few legislatures began to understand that courts could not operate with all volunteer staffs, and they provided for paid professional staff to work with the juveniles and the court. Where they functioned well, such as the Boston Juvenile Court, they fulfilled the 1938 Standards' mandate of providing useful information about a juvenile and his family. However, in 1958, according to a study conducted by the Department of Health, Education, and Welfare, only eight states recognized the role of the probation officer; 55%f the courts hearing children's cases had no probation officers on staff; of those, only one probation officer in ten had special training.

The ambiguous position of the probation officer highlighted basic questions that leaders and citizens had not yet answered: Is the juvenile court a court for juveniles, or is it part of the community's system of services for families in trouble? How could one court serve two contradictory needs: protection of the public interest and the best interest of the child? By the close of the fifties, it was clear that the juvenile court was failing, regardless of which of the above questions was used as a measure. The rapid rise of juvenile delinquency had overwhelmed the system, recidivism was high, and a profound violation of due process rights was underway.

What is due process and why is it important?

Due process evolved in English civil and criminal courts as a more reliable method of arriving at the truth than trial by ordeal, a favorite of the medieval church. It answers the question, what is fair? Essential elements are: notice that a charge has been filed; the right to be heard in a court of law; the right to appeal; in twentieth-century America, the right to be represented by counsel in all criminal proceedings; the privilege against self-incrimination; and, again, in criminal proceedings, the right to be heard by a jury. Due process also guarantees obedience to the rules of evidence. The rules of evidence are intended to guarantee that if an allegation cannot be proved, it cannot be used against the defendant in court.

None of these rights and guarantees was part of Chancery Court procedures. Further, the juvenile court continued to treat both delinquent children and neglected children under the same jurisdictional mandate. The elements of "crime" and "punishment," which had historically been part of the court's authority when it removed abused and neglected children from parents' care under *parens patriae,* could now easily merge with its ungoverned treatment of juvenile delinquents. This produced a situation in which delinquents, abused children, poor children, and their parents were equally subjected to the judicial chaos of the juvenile courts.

This lack of structure was exacerbated by loose definitions. Joel F. Handler, writing in the *Wisconsin Law Review* observed that:

> The statutory definitions of delinquency, dependency, and neglect are so broad that it is hard to imagine most active adolescents not falling within some part of the definitions. In addition to the usual provision which defines a delinquent as one who violates any local, state, or federal criminal law, one finds definitions such as association with "vicious or immoral" persons, "incorrigible," running away from home "without just cause," "beyond control of parent or guardian," using vile, obscene or vulgar language, "disorderly," given to sexual irregularities," or "so deports himself as willfully to injure or endanger the morals of himself or others." The definitions of dependency and neglect are equally broad. A

youth is dependent or neglected if he is "destitute, homeless, or abandoned" or "has a home which by reasons of neglect, cruelty, or depravity on the part of its parents...is an unfit place" or "has not proper parental care or guardianship."

The Setting

Counties usually organize juvenile courts. In 1957, there were approximately 3,000 such courts. They handled 603,000 juveniles, aged ten through seventeen. There was an enormous variety in the structure and procedures for the administration of juvenile justice.

The great majority of juvenile cases did not even reach the court. They started and ended at the police level. The policeman dealt with the juvenile and his family, fashioned his own kind of probation, and became the probation officer/social worker in charge of keeping the juvenile on the straight and narrow path.

In some county jurisdictions, the trial judge simply announced that the court was now sitting as a juvenile court. The judges sitting in these courts had no special training for handling problems of delinquency, dependency, neglect, or domestic difficulty. In most of the county courts there were no probation staffs and no separate detention facilities or hearing rooms.

When cases were brought to court, a variety of informal procedures were put in place. In some cases, probation officers received information from the police and made dispositional decisions. In others, "referees" were used as judge-substitutes. They would hear the less important cases, like those dealing with girls, young boys, or dependent and neglected children. They made their determinations and informed the judge, who then entered an order. These cases were rarely contested. Almost invariably, neither the adolescents nor their parents were represented by counsel.

The issue of the privacy of hearings was also a subject of bitter controversy. Juvenile Justice Standards had called for a closed courtroom and a private hearing, considered to be in the best interest of the child. The open courtroom, with the invariable crowd of curious onlookers, seemed to be the antithesis of the kind of quiet, therapeutic atmosphere for which the juvenile court reformers were searching. Privacy was very seldom achieved, and over time reformers withdrew their demand for it. They began to understand that a private hearing was a fertile breeding ground for abuse—a potential for bullying the uninformed, a potential for unbridled and unintelligent self-righteousness on the part of a judge, a potential for decisions that violate the fairness essential to court proceedings, a potential for tyranny in the guise of brightness and light. Nobody came forth with a solution to this dilemma.

The inconsistency and the underlying threat of overly-harsh punishment, randomly administered, was highlighted by the utter inability of governors and administrators to secure appointments of good juvenile judges. Judges who sat in county courts were appointed for a variety of reasons, *none* of which had to do with their interest in juvenile justice. These judges possessed unbridled discretion. Their orders could send an adolescent from his home to a reform school that amounted to little more than a prison. Albert Deutsch, in his book, *Our Forgotten Children*, described the institutions to which juveniles were sentenced. He said it was not uncommon for juveniles to be housed in cellblocks, guarded by men who controlled them with violence. Parents, poor and uneducated, had no means of appeal.

Theories of what was the best environment for a child infected judges the same way these theories infected the rest of society; most of the judges employed in the juvenile courts merely mirrored the judgments of the class from which they came. It was easy for them to believe that a juvenile brought before them needed some kind of correction, and they did not investigate closely what kind of correctional institute they were sending them to. The United States Children's Bureau reported that between 1955–1960 over one-half of the children judged delinquent had been brought to court on charges of minor misconduct such as carelessness, mischief, truancy, running away, or "ungovernability." The conclusion drawn by critics of the court was that delinquency was defined by the youth's failure to live up to the judge's moral code.

As the Eisenhower administration wound down its last days, observers of the juvenile court system concluded that a system that placed such unfettered power in the hands of even the most well meaning administrators could not be trusted. They called for a reintroduction, in varying degrees, of adversary procedures.

Unknown to juvenile court observers, the Supreme Court would, in four short years, deliver a decision as important in the development of juvenile rights as *Brown v. Board of Education* was in equal education rights.

CHAPTER SEVEN

SOCIAL WELFARE POLICY

1960–2000

CHAPTER SEVEN

Social Welfare Policy

1960–2000

Introduction

The five presidents from John F. Kennedy to William Jefferson Clinton left their mark on modern America's social welfare policies. Public attitude toward welfare vacillated between a general acknowledgement of need and acceptance of programs during the presidency of Lyndon Baines Johnson to bitter rejection during the terms of Ronald Reagan and William Jefferson Clinton. The themes that animated discussion of policy did not change. Should recipients receive direct cash distribution, in-kind services, or both? Should there be a needs test or simply an application from the potential recipient? Should programs be centrally administered by the federal government or locally through cities and towns? Should welfare be a guaranteed right or an annual line item in the budget, requiring Congress to fund it anew every year? Should welfare be conditioned on the recipient's pursuing job counseling or training? Should there be a "cap," a maximum number of years a person could receive welfare? Should exceptions be permitted under the cap?

Neither recession, nor prosperity, nor the political affiliation of the reigning president, nor the presence or absence of a foreign entanglement seems to predict public acceptance or rejection of welfare. Strong presidential leadership, the slant given to the recipients by the news media, and relative prosperity point the way toward acceptance, but do not guarantee it.

A review of the material presented in the next chapters, covering the critical issues of social welfare policy, child protection, social service agencies, and courts will tell us whether we begin the twenty-first century closer to or further from justice at the city gate.

President John F. Kennedy
1960–1963

By 1960, the optimism of the post war era had begun to fade. A series of recessions had begun as far back as 1948, each lasting about a year. After each recession, the economy bounced back, but with less than full vigor. Indeed, each period of recovery was less energetic than the one before it. A renewed and growing concern with unemployment developed during the last years of Eisenhower, when unemployment rates approached 7%.

Poverty, as a relevant political issue, took on a new life as a result of three events that followed in rapid succession: The first was Robert Kennedy's genuine shock at the poverty he observed while campaigning with his brother in rural West Virginia and terribly depressed areas of New York City. He was moved by the misery he saw and lobbied his brother to "do something." Then, the Social Security Administration (SSA) issued reports on poverty based on 1959 census data. The SSA established a poverty index that, for the first time, provided a statistical measure of individual and groups in poverty. Poverty was more pervasive than previously thought. Finally, Michael Harrington's widely read *The Other America* (said to have been read by President Kennedy) and Dwight MacDonald's *Our Invisible Poor* vividly illustrated the poverty hidden in the cities and among the aged and the rural poor.

The first legislation to address these problems was directed at the specific conditions of the depressed areas. The Area Redevelopment Act of 1961 focused on regional unemployment. Its goal was to introduce new industry to areas marginalized by advanced technology or emigration.

In May 1961, Abraham Ribicoff, the new Secretary of Health, Education, and Welfare, appointed an ad hoc Committee on Public Welfare to study the "problems and prospects for public assistance in the next decade." Basic to the committee's proposals were adequate financial assistance to needy persons and families. The committee wrote, "Financial assistance to meet people's basic needs for food, clothing, and shelter is essential, but alone is not enough. *Expenditures for assistance not accompanied by rehabilitation services may actually increase dependency* (emphasis is the author's) and eventual costs to the community." Based on this report and two others (dealing with the Children's Bureau and the Bureau of Public Assistance), Ribicoff proposed a series of changes in public welfare programs. Along with locating deserting fathers and detecting fraud, the changes were designed to "promote rehabilitation services and develop a family-centered approach." The programs were to be developed by the states, each one devising its own plan.

On February 1, 1962, President Kennedy delivered a message to Congress entirely devoted to public welfare, the first such message in American history. He expressed his concern about the existence of poverty in the midst of abundance and stated his belief that *the reasons were more social than economic:*

> Merely responding with a relief check to complicated or personal problems…is not likely to provide a lasting solution. Such a check must be supplemented, or in some cases made unnecessary by positive services and solutions offering the total resources of the community to meet the local needs of the family to help our less fortunate citizens help themselves.

Congress adopted his public welfare recommendations. They became President Kennedy's most important achievement in the field of public welfare. The amendments provided generous funding to the states for their own programs and offered federal money for services not only to current recipients of public assistance but to those who were at risk of becoming public recipients. Aid to Families with Dependent Children was greatly extended. By providing for community work and training programs, the amendments attempted to heed the president's suggestion that work be constructive, with an emphasis on developing new skills. He instructed the planners to include arrangements for the care and protection of children during their parents' absence.

The Kennedy administration, brief though it was, funded projects for the prevention and treatment of delinquency in inner-city neighborhoods including Mobilization for Youth, increased the minimum wage, authored a new housing act to create both housing and construction jobs, led Congress to pass water pollution and control measures, and acquired seashore properties to protect them from depredation. To stimulate consumer buying and corporate investment, Kennedy cut personal and corporate income taxes. The success of this program handed Lyndon B. Johnson a more solidly prosperous economy than Kennedy had inherited from Eisenhower.

Lyndon B. Johnson
1963–1968

By 1964, a more vigorous attack on poverty seemed necessary. President Johnson sought to extend and enlarge Kennedy's programs. One factor that influenced his thinking was the continuing, seemingly uncontrollable increase in AFDC recipients. In December 1964, a total of one million families, including three million children, received assistance. Moreover, the Council of Economic Advisors was using increasingly sophisticated methods to identify the location and number of the poor. Their carefully researched findings were difficult to dismiss. The Council concluded that poverty engulfed about one-fifth of the American people.

In his State of the Union Message in January 1964, Johnson called upon Congress to enact a thirteen-point domestic program that would declare "unconditional war on poverty," a "domestic enemy that threatens the strength of our Nation and the welfare of our people." Finally, "Today, for the first time in our history, we have the power to strike away the barriers to full participation in our society. Having the power, we have the duty." There is every reason to believe that President Johnson meant what he said.

In a White House ceremony on August 24, 1964, the President signed into law the Economic Opportunity Act (EOA), establishing the Office of Economic Opportunity (OEO), the keystone of his "war on poverty." He used seventy-two pens, which he handed out to the notables who had gathered. It was a moment of high drama in which a number of new, important, controversial programs were infused into American public life. The war on poverty was part of the Great Society Program, which also included the most notable civil rights bill in a century, manpower laws, a vastly expanded education bill, Medicare and Medicaid, and other pieces of legislation signaling a slight turn of the wheel of state to the left. The visionary leader and the public perception of need had come together to form *social policy.*

Johnson picked Sargent Shriver to head the OEO. He had been a strikingly successful administrator of the Peace Corps, and, even more appealing to Johnson, he was outside the usual rank-and-file group of bureaucrats, and was directly responsible to him. The various provisions of OEO were legislated separately and always referred to by their titles.

Thus, Titles III and IV provided for special programs to combat poverty in rural areas and for programs of employment and investment incentives in poverty areas beyond the reach of the Area Redevelopment Act. Specifically, loans for small businesses and new investment were to be made available for first-time entrepreneurs. Title V was the Job Corps described above plus a special program for unemployed parents that might be described as "AFDC Plus." It was advertised as a program that not only offered job training but kept families together and "brightened a community." An important section created an adult volunteer corps—Volunteers in Service to America (VISTA)—to help rehabilitate slums and other impoverished areas.

The youth programs included federally-funded Job Corps training centers for out-of-school and unemployed youths who needed general and vocational education; a work training program supporting state and local government and private nonprofit activities aimed at preventing school dropouts; and a work-study program for young people to continue their education in secondary schools, colleges, and universities.

The most controversial and perhaps most important provisions of the Economic Opportunity Act were included in "Urban and Rural Community Action Programs (CAP)." CAP programs promised progress toward the elimination of poverty, providing for the "maximum feasible participation" of the members of the communities targeted. The initial popularity of the OEO stemmed from its ability to get government money directly into the hands of community organizers, without first funneling it through city halls or traditional large-scale charities, such as the United Fund. Among the more popular programs were Head Start, Upward Bound, day-care centers, neighborhood recreation centers, and neighborhood heath centers.

The Community Action Program (and the OEO) came under vigorous attack from widely disparate points. Advocates of the poor called it less a war on poverty than a minor skirmish, a 'sitzkrieg,' a phony war of stalemate and standstill," according to one scholar, and "a war that was declared but never fought," according to another. In fact, in a pattern that would become all too familiar, it was inadequately financed. *Congress appropriated less money each year to combat poverty across the country than was necessary to finance an adequate welfare program in any one of the nation's leading cities.* During the first year of the act's operation, when mayor John Lindsay said that New York City alone needed $10 billion annually for five years to solve its welfare problems, Congress allocated around $750 million (or approximately $30) for each needy citizen for the entire nation.

Moreover, the money was squandered. On the one hand, there were far too many inexperienced community organizers who knew nothing about bookkeeping, and on the other hand, there was a host of infuriated mayors who lost control of their city and their patronage because the federal government bypassed them in its distribution of the funds. The mayors fought, and finally succeeded, to get the funds back into their respective City Halls, where it became business as usual for the friends of the mayor. This led Chicago activist Saul Alinsky to call the program a "macabre masquerade."

Legal suits brought by government-funded community legal services against government entities agitated members of Congress. The aggressiveness and hostility of the poor, who had found the voice to participate—and loudly—shook communities. Stories of mismanagement by local "leaders," radicalism, fraud, and even violence in the job-training camps, abounded.

In time, Lyndon Johnson, increasingly enmeshed in the Vietnam War, became disenchanted with a War on Poverty; it was costly and it created political and social dissension. In late 1966, Johnson's administration began to dismember the OEO, a process continued by Richard M. Nixon when he came into office.

A program so large in concept and so disappointing in its failure was bound to generate streams of commentary. Some commentators observed that a period of intense urban unrest followed the demise of this program, and attribute it to the bitter disappointment that urban dwellers felt when they did not get the promised jobs and assistance. However, a more positive evaluation would include the following: the "maximum feasible participation" concept (derided by Daniel Patrick Moynihan as "Maximum Feasible Misunderstanding") opened up new sources of psychological, financial, and political power to those blacks imprisoned in the ghetto by racial prejudice. Movement into government jobs enabled them to escape poverty and enabled many of them to enter the middle class. In time, they created a black managerial class. Further, this first attempt at real community participation, chaotic as it was, pointed the way to later programs like the Model Cities legislation of 1966.

Of all the programs that affected poor communities, none were greater than community legal services. Although not specifically mentioned in the Economic Opportunity Act, it became clear that the community action programs needed legal assistance achieve their goals. The Legal Assistance

Corporation (LAC) was born, funded by OEO money. This agency, more than any other, wrought changes in the lives of the poor. Pioneering the class-action suit, the LAC changed landlord-tenant relations, corporate behavior, and even departments in the government. It became a hero to the poor and a devil to the more conservative state administrators. The California LAC successfully sued the government of California while Ronald Reagan was governor. When he won the presidency, he said that the first thing he was going to do was end the LAC. While he was unable to "end" it, Congress, under his leadership repeatedly slashed its budget and forbade it to undertake class-action suits or to sue the government.

As his presidency was winding down, the President coaxed and cajoled Congress into doubling the number of people who qualified for food stamps. The administration had a strong internal ally for this program: the Secretary of Agriculture enthusiastically endorsed it, knowing that if more people bought more food, farmers' incomes would increase. The program was very popular—in the South as well as the North. As one commentator observed, "Americans are always in favor of feeding people." By 1993, about 10.5% of the population was using food stamps.

Among the major beneficiaries of the Johnson era were the elderly. On July 30, 1965, the president signed into law the Medicare amendments to the Social Security Act. It was a victory over the American Medical Association and its allies, who relentlessly lobbied against it. The measure represented the nation's first (and very belated) stride toward some sort of national health insurance scheme, at least for more than twenty million of its older citizens. In brief, Medicare provided hospital and medical insurance as well as coverage for some post-hospital care for virtually all Americans upon reaching age sixty-five. The *hospital* insurance was compulsory and financed by an increase in

Social Security taxes, while enrollment in the *out-patient* medical plan was voluntary and paid for by a monthly premium of three dollars (and general tax revenues).

The year 1965 was rounded out with a rent supplement program, funds provided for schools under the Elementary and Secondary School Act and the Higher Education Act, and finally, in 1966, the Model Cities Act.

Neither Kennedy's Public Welfare Amendments nor Johnson's War on Poverty, however, succeeded in getting people off the relief rolls and on to the tax rolls. Indeed, the number of recipients and total expenditures continued to climb. First, the numbers: between 1950 and 1960 (the Eisenhower Administrations), expenditures increased by 92% to over $1 billion. AFDC rolls more than doubled, going from 2.9 million to 7.3 million. Expenditures had risen from slightly over $1 billion in 1960 to $10.3 billion in 1970. Over the ten-year period from 1961 to 1971, the average monthly AFDC stipend increased by $66 in real dollars to $183.

What explains this startling explosion of relief? Begin with the internal migration of twenty million blacks over a thirty-year period from the rural South to the urban North, one of the greatest mass dislocations in American history. These black Americans, who had been marginally employed in Southern agriculture, were rapidly dismissed from their "employment" as the South moved into the modern world of mechanical, labor-free agriculture. They arrived unschooled and unskilled in the cities of the North. They faced powerful racial hostility that cut a swath through their lives in housing, schooling, and employment. In these years, the need for unskilled labor was undergoing a steady, relentless decline. For the second generation of European immigrants, still dependent on employment at the local factories, the numerous factory closings left them, like the black migrants from the

South, in need of government assistance. The common grab for the same scarce jobs contributed to the growing racism of the urban North.

The rise in welfare can also be attributed to people learning for the first time what they were legally entitled to. In the three years between 1966 and 1969, OEO spent about $85 million on legal services. Some 250 legal service projects were established in about 850 neighborhood law offices staffed by about 1,800 lawyers. Many of the legal actions taken by local offices involved obtaining services for clients to which they were entitled, but with regard to which they had previously been ignorant of, or denied.

The poverty statistics at the close of the Johnson era stand as follows: The percentage of Americans living below the poverty line had gone from 22.4% of the population in 1959 to 12.2% in 1969. The poverty line in 1967 was defined as an annual income of $3,100 for an urban family of four, $2,190 for a farm family. These figures represented 9.5% of the white population and 31.1% of the non-white population. These numbers tell us two things: the number of citizens living in poverty was cut in half, and the threshold that defined poverty was very low.

Richard M. Nixon
1968–1975

Richard M. Nixon won a landslide election in November 1968. He had campaigned against radicals, welfare cheats, and social policy planners who wanted to bankrupt the country. He and his political advisers appeared to be a long line of corporate executives with private jets, about as far removed from urban poverty as men could be while still inhabiting the same planet. The electorate that voted him into office was angry: civil rights for blacks seemed to mean riots and destruction; the war in Vietnam split communities and families; the women's movement had rattled both genders, proclaiming an equality that very few people had even considered in the thousands of years before 1960. "Liberal" politics and its causes went into hiding. The poor, once again, were proclaimed the enemy of every working family, taking hard-earned tax dollars for drink and drugs. Nixon reaped the rewards of America's 1960s frustration and trauma.

It may come as a surprise, therefore, to read the evaluation offered by noted policy analyst Sar Levitan. "The greatest extensions of the modern welfare system were enacted under the conservative presidency of Richard Nixon…dwarfing in size and scope the initiatives of John F. Kennedy's New Frontier and Lyndon Baines Johnson's Great Society." Walter I. Trattner adds, "Indeed, while spending for various poverty programs had increased by $27 billion (in 1968 dollars) during the Kennedy-Johnson administrations, it nearly doubled that amount during Nixon's years at the White House."

The newly-elected president relied heavily on Daniel Patrick Moynahan's[8] formulations. Moynihan shared enough of Nixon's dislike for the intellectual

---

[8] Daniel Patrick Moynihan served Presidents Kennedy, Johnson, and Nixon as an adviser in social policy, sometimes drafting the various anti-poverty measures they proposed. He eventually became a senator, representing New York until his retirement in 2000. Senator Moynihan died on March 26, 2003.

elite of the East Coast and enough of Nixon's suspicions of the "social work bureaucracy" to win his trust. Moynihan had an ambitious plan for that welfare policy. It should move, he believed, toward a guaranteed annual income, creating something that resembled a Western European social democracy, with full employment and family allowances. He persuaded Nixon that if the government simply gave poor people money—an income strategy instead of a services strategy—this would end the period of legitimizing, empowering, and enriching social activists, community organizers, civil rights leaders, and the like. So far, Nixon was with him 100%. Further, Moynihan argued, the vast hodgepodge of government social programs could be consolidated into one simple grant. This appealed to Nixon's practical side. The clincher for Nixon was his insight that spending could have a salutary side effect; at the time of civic instability, domestic expenditures could calm an agitated populace.

Nixon revealed his administration's plans for welfare reform in a speech to Congress on August 11, 1969. He boldly proposed to replace AFDC and unemployment insurance with a Family Assistance Plan (FAP), "For those American Families who cannot care for themselves in whichever state they live." It included a negative income tax mechanism that was designed to set a floor on income while still encouraging people to work. It reduced a morass of regional variation by guaranteeing minimum income with *uniform national standards.*

Nixon grounded his plan in an *income* strategy as opposed to a *services* strategy. Kennedy had tried *programs* and banned the delivery of money payments; Johnson had tried both *programs* and *cash;* now Nixon proposed an *income (cash)* plan, with no mention at this point of a *program.* Furthermore, the federal government was to administer the payments. By shifting the burden of payments from the states and localities to the federal government, he could destroy the network of the despised bureaucrats, social workers, community organizers, political activists, and civil rights leaders. From a political point of view, this bold move, made early in his administration, would preempt the Democrats, whose leadership was contemplating some proposals of their own. Because he regarded this as an innovation in federal-state funding and welfare programming, he called his program the New Federalism.

The plan failed in Congress by eight votes. Conservatives noted with displeasure that Nixon's proposal eliminated eligibility requirements. (Where's the all-important demeaning means test?) Further, Nixon took control out of the hands of local government and brought administration back to the hated Washington. Liberals regarded the benefit levels as appallingly low, so they did not support the bill. In the end, Nixon lost interest in it. Moynihan, self-defined as a Democrat and a liberal, could not understand the liberals' rejection of the bill on the basis that the benefits were too low. He said in disgust, "Liberals shoot for the stars, and lose everything."

Congress did pass a Comprehensive Childcare Act that would have provided billions of federal dollars for preschool, day care, nutritional and other programs, but Nixon vetoed it. He believed that it would encourage parents to abdicate their responsibilities, removing the family from its "rightful position as the keystone of our civilization." This remains, perhaps, the most enduring conservative reflex of political leaders. One has only to think back to the extraordinary rhetoric that congressmen used to oppose the first Children's Bureau, or to the extension of the day-care programs that had been so successful during W.W.II.

However, Nixon acceded to the pressure coming from his Democratic Congress on a significant number of progressive measures. In 1970, he signed the Occupational Safety and Health Act, a statute that significantly increased federal oversight of safety and health standards. In 1972, he approved the Local

Fiscal Assistance Act, called revenue-sharing, which provided federal block grants to the localities for various social programs, including low-income housing, expanded federal rent subsidies, and job training. He consented to Congress' decision to raise Social Security benefits by 20%.

Further, in 1972, Nixon joined with Congress to expand and improve the Food Stamp Program. He made the program mandatory for the states and allowed recipients with no earned income to receive stamps without having to make cash payments, thereby allowing millions of impoverished families to purchase food in quantities not possible with their meager welfare checks. The Food Stamp Program also provided funds for child nutrition and rent subsidies. Food stamp expenditure rose from $550 million in 1970 to $4.4 billion in 1975—an eightfold increase—and more than doubled again in 1981, to $10 billion. The public approved. As previously observed, over the course of history, hunger has moved Americans more than any other form of deprivation.

Nixon triumphed again with another landslide election in 1972. During his campaign he repeatedly denounced the Johnson-era big spenders, accusing them of undermining hard-working Americans, pandering to social workers, and coddling criminals. He called for reductions in government services and expenditures.

He then proceeded (perhaps alert citizens could have predicted this) to confound everybody. While he placed many anti-welfare conservatives in office and often impounded funds appropriated by Congress for various social programs, he also approved passage of another host of costly measures designed to help needy citizens, that is, the "*deserving* needy" citizens, such as the permanently disabled, the elderly, and the working poor. Hence, he signed into law the 1973 Rehabilitation Act according physically-disabled persons protection from discrimination, and he signed legislation that established the Earned

Income Tax Credit. This is comparable to a negative tax; it that provided families with dependent children who earned $4,000 a year or less a refundable tax credit of 10% of their income, to be administered through the Internal Revenue Service as part of the annual tax collection process. For the first time in its history, America used the tax system as a mechanism to provide resources to the needy. This law provides for a steady increase to keep up with inflation and has been a genuine gift to the beleaguered working poor.

Subsequently, Nixon signed into law the Comprehensive Employment and Training Act, or CETA, which subsidized hundreds of thousands of public service jobs, without a means test. This was the second time Nixon proposed a piece of social policy legislation that did not require a means test and was being offered to applicants above the poverty line. This time the conservatives in Congress did not block its passage. Perhaps that was because the legislation creating it turned administration of the program back to the states, a priority for conservative Congressmen, who were deeply suspicious of the federal government.

Nixon also approved the indexing of Social Security and SSI—to make automatic "cost-of-living adjustments" (COLA) in these benefits. In 1975, his administration adopted the Supplemental Security Income Program, which federalized all public assistance programs for the adult unemployable poor, thus creating created the nation's first guaranteed-income program. SSI is an "entitlement;" it is a preferred social welfare program because it is "locked in," and not subject to the discretion of some administrator or the whim of Congress.

The decades between 1960 and 1980 continued to bring segments of the population into the mainstream; the proportion of elderly poor fell from 35% of the population to 16%. In 1963, one of every five Americans living in poverty had never seen a doctor. By 1970, that figure dropped to 8%, and the proportion visiting a physician annually was about the same as anyone else. Between 1965 and 1972, infant mortality dropped 33%. Food stamps successfully reduced hunger. Housing programs lessened overcrowding and the number of people living in substandard housing. Operation Headstart helped significant numbers of poor children prepare for school; Upward Bound prepared large numbers of adolescents for college; low cost loans permitted thousands of young people with low or modest incomes to attend college. Legal Services expanded the rights of the poor by using class-action suits in key areas: medical aid, landlord-tenant relations, state housing laws, consumer credit, and welfare administration. (Recall that Legal Services could not survive the wrath of Ronald Reagan and has almost disappeared from the political map.).

A stroll through any major city in 1975 would alert the walker to the sights and smells of poverty. One would notice the disintegrating housing, the pot-holed streets, the empty lots strewn with broken glass, the uncollected garbage. But we must acknowledge the two decades for what they achieved. The number of people living below the poverty line was cut in half through Medicare, Medicaid, food stamps, rent subsidies, vast increases in Old Age Insurance, and significant amendments to the Social Service Act that reached out to include the physically and mentally disabled. The black middle class benefited greatly from the War on Poverty. The Great Society generated an unprecedented number of social service jobs, bringing 850,000 blacks into full-time employment and tripling the size of the black middle class.

For those concerned that these programs were too expensive for our nation to sustain, there is the following revealing statistic: the Economic Opportunity

Act of 1964 cost the federal government $15.5 billion, less than a seventh of the $120 billion the federal government spent on the Vietnam War.

Were the leaders of War on Poverty guided by a desire to ameliorate deprivation in American society? Or, in a less altruistic vein, were programs shaped by men competing to gain glory for themselves? Did highly political men who saw their chance to look like heroes advance programs? Was everything designed to keep the restive blacks quiet? What if the answer to all the questions is Yes? Consider that the legislative agenda advanced by Presidents Kennedy, Johnson, and Nixon broke new ground in securing a place for the government in people's lives and brought America closer to considering poverty a national responsibility. The public did not always thank them for this, but history should.

Jimmy Carter
1976–1980

President Ford, the President who briefly succeeded Richard Nixon, had never evinced interest in social policy during his many years in the Senate. He carried this indifference into his brief tenure at the White House. Ford proposed no social welfare legislation, and none was passed.

Jimmy Carter was very different from his immediate predecessors. His appeal was that he was an old-fashioned populist who felt for the common folk; he also possessed a clearly articulated human-rights ideology. Unfortunately, during his during his term gas prices soared, cutting revenue to the government. Since there appeared to be a need for increased spending by the military, the shortfall in revenue was taken out of the social welfare budget.

Carter was also caught in an economic trend not of his making, but destined to plague not only his presidency but also that of his successor, Ronald Reagan. The years between 1970 and 1990 witnessed an acceleration in the shift from an industrial to a service economy, which had begun in the Eisenhower years. During these two decades, employment increased by 2% in the manufacturing sector and 92% in the service sector. Factory employment, bearing the brunt of economic dislocation, declined, taking down with it the last of the unskilled, blue-collar workers this country had once relied on. The loss of present and future jobs in the old industrial communities ("the rust belt") brought financial insecurity to white workers and devastation to blacks, who would never be able to make up for this loss in employment in the new service economy. The new service economy offered lower wages, part-time and seasonal work, and provided no health insurance, or government guaranteed benefits, the latter dependent on full-time work.

Carter had a few successes. He was able to create a cabinet post for the Department of Energy. He managed to get several pieces of legislation that aided the nation's youth, such as the National Youth Employment Bill, and a measure designed to rescue children from longtime stays in foster homes. He obtained passage of a bill expanding Medicare and the rights of the disabled. He attempted a genuine overhaul of welfare, dubbed the "Better Jobs and Income Program." It failed in Congress, as did his suggestion about how to make Social Security more secure and his plan for universal health insurance.

As the 1980 election approached, Americans focused on what they regarded as his failures: the Iran hostage crises (then over a year old), the Soviet Union's invasion of Afghanistan, and the overwhelmingly bad economic news; the nation was in a deep hole of double-digit inflation. When he left office in 1980, Carter had a 21% approval rating, the lowest of any president in recent memory.

Ronald Reagan and George H. W. Bush
1980–1988, 1988–1992

Jimmy Carter's successor was Ronald Reagan. Relying on folksy and nostalgic rhetoric, Ronald Reagan, the champion of no government, no payments to the poor, extensive aid to corporations, and billions for the Strategic Defense Initiative (Star Wars), swept into the office of the presidency. Reagan knew who the enemy of the average, hard-working American was; it was the welfare cheat, the freeloader. The public cried, "Yes!" and gave him the presidency and the Republican Party control of the Senate. His cabinet became a businessmen's cabinet, and his economic plan became the business of rewarding "supply-side economics." Supply-side economics was, in a frank aside uttered by Reagan's own director of the Office of Management and Budget, David Stockman, a Trojan horse filled with gifts for the rich. It was a thinly disguised version of the already failed "trickle down" theory.

Here is the supply-side story: Keep production and prices high. Do this with a large tax cut for the producing classes. They will invest their profits, and there will be jobs for everyone. However, the wealthy did not invest their newfound money in jobs-creating enterprises. They invested it in foreign banks, or in goods that might have been profitable to them but irrelevant to the production of consumer goods.

Reagan's tax cut for corporations had two results. First, the rich gained in income and the poor lost. Families with incomes of over $100,000 received a tax cut of $9,000 and the poorest one-fifth of Americans received a tax *increase* of 22.7% of their income. Second, since the cuts produced neither increase in investment nor the production of affordable goods, government revenue fell, producing the highest budget deficit in American history.

With the decline of the GNP came a continuing attrition of jobs. The median family income grew very slowly. The gap between the very rich and the very poor grew markedly: the number of billionaires quadrupled during the eighties at the same time that the number of people falling below the poverty line increased by 35%. The "misery index"—the sum of the inflation rate and the unemployment rate, grew all through the two Reagan administrations. Seeing the decline of the GNP, the high unemployment rate, the virtual collapse of the steel and auto industries, accumulating business failures, and thousands of people lined up at soup kitchens, Wall Street financiers and his own advisors urged Reagan to reverse his course. Reagan ignored them. He went ahead with his scheduled tax cuts, increased military spending, and slashed welfare budgets.

He terminated all programs for the unemployed (including CETA, a Republican jobs program under Nixon), took billions out of the programs for school lunch, food stamps, subsidized housing, energy assistance, family planning, public and mental-health services, alcohol and drug counseling, legal aid (a favorite enemy), the Job Corps, and, of course, AFDC. He gave this money to the military. When he was finished, federal expenditure for these social welfare programs constituted less than 1% of the federal budget. Defense consumed well over 25% of the budget.

Bodies littered the floor. Eliminating CETA threw 400,000 new unemployed into the labor market. The 400,000 or so people who lost their AFDC also lost their food stamps and Medicaid. Reducing Women and Infant Children (WIC) by 30% was especially brutal. It affected the health of 700,000 children. The Center for Communicable Diseases, the government's medical research arm, reported that WIC programs had made dramatic improvements in child health, reducing poverty-related maladies like low birth weight, anemia, and physical and mental retardation. Many in the medical community protested the cuts, but to no avail. Then there was the matter of hunger. The Physician Task Force on Hunger in America issued a report in 1985 stating,

> Hunger is a national health epidemic. It is our judgment that the problem of hunger in America is now more widespread and serious than at any time in the last ten to fifteen years....We believe that hunger, dealt a serious blow by the programs of the late sixties and seventies, has returned. It is a serious problem across the nation and in every region of the nation. We have, in fact, returned from no city and no state where we did not find extensive hunger.

Five hundred thousand people were removed from SSI. Social Security Income, normally regarded as an entitlement, was not supposed to be questioned. This was akin to eliminating Social Security from 500,000 retired people. Many of those removed were mentally ill, diagnosed with unremediable problems like schizophrenia. Reagan decided they could work for a living. Finally, Robert M. Hayes, a former Wall Street lawyer who was head of the National Coalition for the Homeless, reported that a new wave of destitute citizens could be found in the nation's streets—some 60,000—many of whom were children and infants.

Reagan remained steadfast. A group of religious leaders representing all faiths and denominations chastised him for budget priorities that revealed a "nation intent on a selfish and dangerous course of social stinginess and military overkill" and represented "a real moral failure." He was not moved. Reagan believed (correctly, since he easily won re-election in 1984) that he had the support of the ordinary citizen and was in the good company of his favorite intellectuals (whose writings he did not bother to read). Among those that did the spadework for the Reagan Revolution, none was more popular than the sociologist Charles Murray, author of the controversial book *Losing Ground.* This book, more than any other work at the time, re-packaged the standard view that welfare programs are harmful to the poor. Murray argued that relief policies—especially AFDC, food stamps, and even federal job-training programs—undermine individual responsibility, create a state of dependency, and thus prevent the poor from becoming self-sufficient. By making unemployment "affordable," welfare spending created an environment, or culture, that encouraged dropping out of school at an early age, abandoning low-wage jobs, and having illegitimate children. It thus perpetuated, and even worsened, the poverty problem.

Since this perception refuses to die, let us pause here for a closer look at Aid to Families with Dependent Children (AFDC). The reader will recall that Aid to Dependent Children was a part of the Social Security Act legislation created by the Roosevelt Administration in response to the Great Depression. It was built on the model of the Widows' Pensions of the Progressive Era. That is, it was help for the "worthy poor." Even though payments were kept at subsistence level, and even though the widows' claim seemed legitimate, the press sometimes called the recipients "gilt-edged" widows.

ADC was like the other "alphabet agencies," (i.e., intended to go out of business with the return of prosperity). Roosevelt himself worked very hard to insure that the unemployed were given jobs for pay, because he personally disliked giving cash for no work. In his 1935 State of the Union address, he denigrated his own program, referring to relief as a "narcotic…a subtle destroyer of the human spirit." He concluded that a handout was "in violation of the traditions of America. *Work must be found for able but destitute workers.*"

The other New Deal agencies expired, but ADC (made AFDC in 1950) did not. Rather than go out of business, AFDC took on a life of its own. It became the core of every poverty program between 1945 and 1996. The program continues to struggle with its historical burden. It is never seen as anything but an unearned hand out to the unworthy poor.

AFDC gradually fell under the same combination of paternalism and suspicion as all previous welfare programs between 1630 and 1950. Recipient families were viewed as deficient and in need of wise counsel as well as money. If they were not immoral they were probably lacking in initiative, and alms alone would only make matters worse by rewarding dependency. The need to be punitive was ever present. In short order, "suitable home" rules were put in place, so families found to be neglecting their children would lose their benefits. Great diligence was applied in attempting to root out persons who might be cheating. Investigators went to homes to go through the families' belongings to assess need. They conducted midnight raids to find out if some man who could be supporting the family was living in the home (and to humiliate the couple). These harassments were in time ruled illegal. Although ruled illegal, recipients of AFDC were still viewed as not worthy of aid and not citizens with equal rights.

Still, the welfare rolls continued to grow. Economic historians offer many reasons for this growth. They fall under the heading of "structural" problems; given the unrelenting assault on recipients, these problems deserve, once again, to be enumerated. There is the employment situation. In simple English, a man cannot work if there is no job. The dramatic loss of factory/city jobs severely undermined families' efforts to bring in their own income, true for both black and white families. In addition, the economy had not recovered from the slump of the inflation/gas-hike era. To put a final touch of bitter irony to Reagan's hostility to the jobless, it is now clear that Reagan maintained a *policy* of high unemployment because he thought that would stimulate growth!

The think-tank authors whose writings give voice to the Calvinist view of poverty are not interested in the reasons cited above. They are well aware that federal funding of AFDC is an insignificant portion of the federal budget. That is not important. Rather, they are outraged that the poor continue to exist. Statistics and graphs are a cover for the oldest game in the history of Anglo-Saxon welfare law: find your impoverished victim, pretend that a terrific job is available, and if only he were not lazy, shiftless, lowly, or morally-impaired, he would get it. The problem of poverty, or pauperism, would vanish.

The problem did not vanish for President Reagan. Unemployment continued to rise, the economy was not picking up, and shortly before the 1988 election *Time* Magazine ran a special cover story on "Begging in America," calling on the president to "do something."

Congress had actually been working for months on a welfare reform bill that it hailed as a "sweeping overhaul of the nation's welfare system," making it a job-employment system instead of a payment system. Daniel Patrick Moynihan, now in his reincarnation as a senator from New York, resurrected the old Family Assistance Program, calling it the Family Support Act. The president signed it into law in October 1988, one month before the general election. Its main purpose was to expand work programs linked to welfare. The major provision of the $6.8 billion federal statute—intended to begin 1990 and phase in over a six-year period—was the Job Opportunities and Basic Skills (JOBS) program. It required single mothers with children over the age of three to work or enroll in education or job training courses in order to receive benefits.

The idea of forcing welfare recipients, primarily women with young children, to enter the workforce in return for benefits was hardly novel, nor had it been successful on numerous tries in the past. Furthermore, the statute, like so many previous welfare reform measures, was based on four dubious assumptions—assumptions, in fact, proved incorrect by many of scholarly studies and by the experience of real welfare mothers. These assumptions merit a careful review. The first assumption is that most recipients are on welfare for a long time. In reality, two to three years is the most common term. The second assumption is that women control and manipulate their lives in order to receive welfare. The following, therefore, would be the scenario: a young girl begins a carefully-planned pattern of failing in school. As she becomes a young teenager she perfects her goal of school failure and quits. Then, looking over all the wonderful men available to her, she chooses the one she knows will impregnate her and leave her. Of course, this is a satirical evaluation of the process. Among first-time welfare mothers (if they are teenage school dropouts), research shows that *nothing* in their lives has been planned. They do not think of the future; they do not plan—they drift. The brightest among them will begin to make plans *after* the baby is born.

The third assumption is that welfare families are "very large." Welfare families are currently averaging 2.9 children per family. Finally, the fourth assumption is that they would work if faced with starvation. That is probably true, providing there was some job somewhere. But is it essential that we starve a portion of our population? Both they and their children already deal with poor nutrition on a daily basis, partly out of ignorance, and partly because the welfare money always runs out before the month does. Again, do we really want to have a national policy of "work or starve" for mothers and their children?

Several points about President Reagan's expenditures bear repeating.

- In 1980 and 1981, there were approximately eleven million recipients of welfare in America, seven million of who were children, many under the age of six. Annual federal expenditures for welfare amounted to less than 1% of the federal budget, while defense consumed 25%.

- His fiscal 1983 budget, which included another tax cut that favored the well-to-do and projected a $99 billion deficit, called for a $34 billion dollar increase over the previous year's budget in spending for the military, while cutting another $27 billion in social programs.

- In 1985, a Congress—Watch Lawyer pointed out that Reagan's program of "Corporate Welfare," (tax gimmicks) had cost the U.S. Treasury more than $38 billion in lost revenue.

- The president's pet project, the Strategic Defense Initiative (Star Wars), would cost billion of dollars and, according to many scientists who refused to work on it, would probably never work. In June 2000, the *New York Times* reported that this project had already cost the U.S. $60 billion and had yet to produce a working system.

Ronald Reagan led, and the nation followed. Social service programs lay in tatters. No one can approximate the numbers hurt by these cuts; both recipients and service providers had to make do. And as everyone is aware, "making do" means "doing without."

The president bequeathed to his successor, George H. W. Bush, a staggering $2.6 trillion debt that precluded any major welfare initiatives. This was convenient for Bush, who had no interest in domestic policy. By 1990, the economy was cycling through a serious recession once again. Poverty increased from 12.8% of the population in 1989 to 14.2% in 1991. Unemployment continued to rise at an alarming rate. It included not only the dismissal of the unskilled—for example, 74,000 blue-collar workers laid off at General Motors—but added middle-level bureaucrats and administrators, who were victims of downsizing, such as the 20,000 who lost their jobs at International Business Machine. Sometimes they were the ones who moved into the lower-skilled jobs and booted the working class out. As we have already seen, the number of manufacturing jobs in the nation fell precipitously, abolishing 1.8 million positions between 1981 and 1991. At the same time, the population sixteen and older grew by 19.4 million.

Government fiscal policies exacerbated the growing inequality of wealth. He followed the Reagan prescription of "getting the economy going," even though this prescription had been a noticeable failure for eight years. Once again, government planners were obsessed with balancing the budget, and once again their imaginative way to do so was to cut social service programs. The victims were the usual: food, health, housing, job training, and income programs. And once again, capital gains taxes and taxes for upper income tax payers were cut so they could increase their investments and stimulate growth. To nobody's surprise, they chose not to. Toward the end of his administration Bush began to understand the discontent of the middle class, but he had nothing to offer them. Instead, he used his last State of the Union address in 1992 to attack the welfare system and the recipients of income transfers. He said that aid recipients were responsible for holding their families together and for refraining from having children out of wedlock. By the time Bush left office, income inequality had reached new heights: 5% of the households received 21.2% of the national income. States, feeling the loss of federal contributions to their budgets, had devised new ways to reduce welfare caseloads. New Jersey passed a law withholding new money from women already on welfare who had additional babies. Other states halted their already minimal job training programs. Homelessness was reported to be the worst since the Great Depression. Bush and Congress agreed on a law that that raised the minimum wage from $3.35 an hour to $4.25 an hour. This left a *full-time* worker with a family of four $1,400 *below* the poverty level.

William J. Clinton
1992–2000

The following is a snapshot of America's welfare population when Clinton took office. In 1994, 14.3 million Americans received aid, 9 million of whom were children. One-third of welfare mothers—the largest single group—were between the ages of twenty and thirty-nine. Mothers under age twenty represented 8% of the welfare population. The racial distribution stood at 39% white, 37% black, 18% Hispanic, and 5% "other." The annual welfare budget was $22 billion. Clinton's plan would increase that figure over time by about $9 billion.

Bill Clinton made welfare reform a major theme of his first election campaign. Proud of the welfare-to-work program that he was responsible for as Governor of Arkansas, he wanted to "end welfare as we know it," adding that national health insurance, job training, education, and childcare must be part of the package. He also said that the minimum wage should be increased, and when welfare recipients reached their time limits, if they couldn't find work in the private sector, the public sector should provide a job of last resort. There was little to quarrel with here.

But when, after considerable time had elapsed, Clinton's aides did set forth a welfare bill, supporters were surprised and displeased. The bill seemed to "out-Reagan Reagan." At its core were time caps: no recipient could expect to be on welfare for longer than two years, and had a lifetime maximum of five years. Benefits were clearly tied to the recipient's willingness to be engaged in job training or work. Only women with children under the age of one were exempt.

Since an honest, effective job-training program would be expensive, especially if it included the necessary child-care and transportation funds, the next six months became a search for money. Estimates varied greatly over this period. In January, the administration started with numbers that nobody believed and nobody would allow: $14.5 billion a year to provide job training for 500,000 to a million jobs. It proposed to produce the necessary revenue by taxing food stamps, welfare benefits, and housing assistance, and to cut aid to legal immigrants who were elderly and indigent.

These proposals produced a political firestorm.

When the angry response mounted from the entire welfare community, Clinton's friends, and the Democratic Congress, sought a more acceptable set of proposals. The administration said it would reduce its budget to $9.3 billion over five years. A tax on gambling receipts and the corporate environmental income tax would also produce revenue. But these taxes yielded a paltry income. The president decided that most of the money would be raised by reducing existing programs for low-income people. Democratic opponents in Congress called this "eating our young."

At this time, Clinton's Commission on the Homeless reported seven million homeless Americans. In March 1994, the Census Bureau provided new evidence that the percentage of people working full time but earning less than the poverty level had risen 50% in the last thirteen years. These were employed people who could not lift themselves out of poverty. The continued poverty of the fully employed meant that the goal of the Clinton welfare plan could not be achieved by using jobs to end the need for government aid. The census report also indicated that the income gap was *continuing to widen*, with the top fifth of American households earning 48.2% of the nation's income, *the bottom fifth earning just 3.6%*. Finally, the report revealed the unsettling fact that 30% of all Americans were now born to single mothers; 22% of that number were born to white mothers and 66% to black mothers. Political conservatives said,

"The issue is no longer making welfare recipients work; it is preventing them from having out-of-wedlock births!" Although reformers would normally dismiss this shriek as one more piece of conservative moralizing, they themselves were concerned. Reports and findings over the decades had pointed to single motherhood as an almost certain guarantee of lifelong poverty.

The 431-page Welfare Bill that Clinton submitted to Congress on July 15, 1994, presented the nation with sweeping changes. Knowing this bill was more draconian than he himself had envisioned, his rhetoric was subdued. He accompanied his presentation with the statement that he hoped "the time limits, combined with billions of dollars in new training, work, childcare, and the earned income tax credit program will move recipients into private jobs....Let us be honest," he said. "None of this will be easy to accomplish." advocates were stunned by the severe provisions. Although Clinton claimed to reject a complete cutoff for the non-compliant, he embraced a set of escalating penalties that would culminate in the denial of all cash to a mother who refused to work. The bill allowed states to deny increased payments to women who had additional children. Clinton had moved far to the right, but to conservatives, anticipating victory in the fall elections, no move to the right was far enough. Republican leadership talked about denying all aid to mothers under 21 years of age.

Clinton had yet to determine how to finance his proposals, modest though they were. Clinton, his cabinet, and his host of welfare advisers could think of nothing else but to cut the anti-poverty budget, including $3.7 billion in programs for legal immigrants and $1.6 billion in an emergency program for people at risk of eviction. In total, $7 billion of the $9.3 billion was going to be taken directly from those already battered down, marginalized, powerless, and living on the edge. And the $7 billion was going for a job-training program that Clinton himself had doubts about, because he knew the amount of money was too limited to support real training and he knew, as did every one of his advisors, that the economy had not yet shaken its recession and that unemployment was still high.

On November 8, 1994, Americans went to the polls and voted into office Congressman Newt Gingrich and a very conservative set of Representatives, men who claimed they would *really* end welfare.

For two years, Congress and the Clinton administration bitterly wrangled about the shape of the Welfare Bill. On August 22, 1996, after months of legislative back-and-forth and thousands of hours of wrenching policy debate within the administration itself, the president signed into law The Welfare Reform Reconciliation Act. Thus, AFDC, born sixty-one years ago during the Depression, a perennial object of dispute and disgust, breathed its last. In its place, block grants were to be given to the states for individual state administration. The federal government maintained some rules and guidelines, but gave the states a great deal of latitude about how to spend their money. Public policy had swung back to favoring local control.

The act created a single capped entitlement to states, called Temporary Assistance for Needy Families (TANF). The states' spending was to be limited to families on assistance for five years or less (over a lifetime), subject to a 20% state caseload exemption. The states were required to ensure federally established work participation requirements for their caseloads. No single mother could remain on the rolls longer than two consecutive years without enrolling in school or taking a job. States that did not fulfill federally mandated requirements would lose their share of federal money. The requirement was that 25% of single parent families and 50% of two-parent families must be in work activity within one year, increasing to 50% and 90% by 2002, respectively.

States could exempt a mother with children under five years of age, but a mother could only ask for this exemption once. "Work activity" included subsidized and unsubsidized jobs, on-the-job training, vocational education, or employment training. Individuals in work activities were required to participate twenty hours per week in 1996, increasing to thirty hours a week by 2000.

The reader will note that the conservative end of American politics is currently proclaiming that all mothers, to be morally correct, should stay out of the workplace and in the home raising children, but that welfare mothers, to be morally correct, should be in the workplace, and not in the home raising their children.

The law further required that a single mother had to provide information about the child's missing father or risk losing 25% of her benefits, that unmarried minors live with parents or other adults in a supervised setting (though there was no way to enforce this), and that adults without diplomas be working toward a degree in order to receive benefits.

States were granted the right to cap family benefits when an additional child was born while the family was receiving benefits. (When New Jersey did this, and a Rutgers University study revealed a rise in the number of abortions among welfare mothers, conservatives found themselves trapped in a very uncomfortable dilemma of their own creation). States were permitted to sanction families (i.e., withhold benefits) if their children were truant from school, and to terminate Medicaid if an adult refused to work.

Clinton acknowledged that the bill he was signing reversed six decades of social welfare policy and touched the lives of millions of people. The bill that emerged from Congress would affect most of the 12.8 million people on welfare. It would alter the benefits paid to more than one-fifth of the families with children, "saving" $60 billion over six years, mostly by cutting food stamps and benefits to legal immigrants.

David T. Ellwood, poverty specialist at Harvard University and author of an early version of the Clinton welfare reform bill, subsequently resigned in protest over the shape of the final bill. He wrote in the New York Times, "…the Republican Bill is far more about budget cutting than about putting people to work. Bathed in the rhetoric of reform the bill's authors are more dangerous than most people realize. No bill that is likely to push more than a million additional children into poverty—many in working families—is real reform." He pointed out that a genuine funding of job programs was not cheap. Wisconsin Governor Tommy Thompson was administering a successful job-training program that, contrary to the budget-cutting fantasies of Congressional leadership, cost the state more than welfare. Ellwood continued, "States are getting block grants for welfare and work programs. But the grants for childcare, job training, workfare, and cash assistance *combined* amount to less than $15.00 a week—whom are we kidding?"

Business economist Peter Passell wrote in the *New York Times* that August, "This is reform on a shoe string. Over a five-year period the federal budget will save $15 billion. The states will have to spend much more of their own money, and the conscientious ones are already complaining."

Appropriations to social service agencies were slashed by two-thirds. This may have been one of the most deleterious results of the act. Without money, social-service agencies went "inactive." The federal government dropped all pretense of monitoring or control. Up to 30% of the block-grant money was transferred to more popular programs, such as senior services. Without money to run their programs, social services suffered. At least twenty-one states were under court order for not meeting care-and-protection standards. In many states, child-welfare officials delayed investigating reports of child abuses and neglect, placed children in unsafe foster homes, offered fewer social services to keep families together, and failed to find appropriate adoptive homes. In the decade that just came to a close, the number of children who were reported to be abused or neglected quadrupled. Federal advisory committees called abuse and neglect the leading cause of death among children under the age of four. Since research was beginning to establish a link between economic depravation and abusive behavior of parents, critics of this bill could justifiably say that this administration contributed to child abuse.

The cuts in legal-immigrant services (SSI and food stamps) and the narrowing of disabled children's eligibility for SSI, which removed over 100,000 children from the rolls, seemed particularly cruel since neither had anything to do with welfare provisions, and neither cost the federal government very much money. The immigrants getting SSI were largely non-English-speaking elderly people. Fear and panic gripped the immigrant communities. At first, no appeal was permitted, then it was. But appeal is always a slow process, and a possible, or even a probable reverse order is only marginally helpful. During all that waiting time, both the disabled and the immigrants still had to eat. These immigrant cuts were projected to save the government $22 billion over the succeeding six years.

NOTE: In October 1997, a year after making the cuts, Congress bowed to pressure from the welfare community and ordinary citizens and restored most of the SSI programs for disabled children and legal immigrants.

The second major change produced by this bill was that federal money was now capped. The block grants totaled $164 billion annually for the country, with no new funding for jobs-and-training and placement-and-training efforts. This funding was to stay the same for six years with no adjustment for inflation or population growth.[9]

The time limits stirred further concerns. At any particular time, 20% of the caseload would be represented by people who had been on the rolls over five years. The law did permit this—it permitted each state to carry up to 20% of its caseload beyond the five-year limit. But the welfare community was still anxious. A recent study of the Kaiser Foundation found that 30% of that long-time-welfare group was composed of women who were caring for disabled children or parents, or who were disabled themselves. It should be pointed out here the incidence of disabled adults and children is higher in poor communities, while the resources for care are fewer. A study in the state of Washington showed that 36% of the women in the caseload had learning disabilities that had never been remediated. Also, a little-known fact about women's failure to obtain work was revealed by a survey indicating that a significant number of women who were victims of domestic violence were afraid to go to work because their husbands had threatened them with a beating if they brought home a paycheck. The result of these anomalies left social service workers wondering if they were going to face a cut off of federal funds because their permanent case load was too large for the federal regulations, and not amenable to cuts.

The work-participation requirement seemed particularly threatening. The bill required that the states have a specific percentage of their welfare recipients in jobs or job training by specific dates. States that did not conform would suffer a reduction in federal assistance. All welfare-watchers said that the states

---

[9] This stingy appropriation recalls the 1964 appropriation under President Johnson's War on Poverty grants. Mayor John Lindsay of New York told Congress he needed $10 billion annually for one city for five years to solve the welfare problem. Congress allocated $750 million for the entire nation, or approximately $30.00 for each needy citizen.

could not conform, that *jobs could not be found.* However, an exuberant national economy came to the rescue of Clinton, the states, and the welfare community. By 1996, the country had experienced six years of sustained growth, the longest period of sustained growth since World War II, the unemployment rate steadily dropped to the lowest it had been since the early 1970s, when the Bureau of Labor Statistics first began to keep track. In its need for more workers, companies took the unskilled and trained them. This burst of activity during the nineties kept the threat of "no available work" quiescent.

The flood of single mothers into the robust labor market was the law's single achievement. The question was how much unskilled mothers could achieve once they entered the job market. Few managed to keep full-time jobs all year. While their earnings were up, the growth of their paychecks was largely offset by reductions in welfare and food stamps. Indeed, in economic terms, it was not clear whether the average woman was gaining ground. No one could predict what would happen if the nation experienced one of its cyclical recessions. But in the first years after the bill's adoption, economic growth was strong enough to slightly reduce the income gap between the richest and poorest for the first time in four decades.

However, the changed work environment did not produce a change in the percentage of Americans below the poverty line. The official overall poverty rate was stuck at 13% and the rate of child poverty at 19%. The *Globe*, December 3, 2000, filled in the remainder of the picture: child poverty rates were rising. The poverty rate for children in the three-year period 1993–1995 was 16%; over the three years 1997–1999 the average rate rose to 18%. The percentage of all children in the state of Massachusetts who were very poor (i.e., lived in families whose income fell 50% below the poverty income threshold) rose from 6.5% over the 1993–1995 period to 9.6% in 1997–1999.

Massachusetts entered the fray by adopting policies that were more stringent than the federal government's. An October 1999 study released by the Radcliffe Public Policy Institute said that 80% of the people who were due to be cut from the welfare rolls were caring for children with chronic illnesses. The children required constant medical monitoring. The study added, "Many of the ailments, such as asthma, lead poisoning, and chronic ear infections leading to hearing loss and developmental delays have been found to be more common among children living in poverty. The children really require either their mother's constant attendance or her ability to be near a phone; the phone becomes necessary for a quick consultation if the child is in medical trouble. One mother reported being fired because she was on the phone too often; another said she quit because she had to work as a cleaning woman in a building where she could not be reached by phone." Massachusetts Governor Paul Cellucci responded to these and other problems by saying that he wanted to increase the twenty hours of paid or unpaid work required by the federal government to thirty hours.

To make this situation worse, both the Governor and the legislature stubbornly refused to allow attendance in high-school-equivalency classes or in junior colleges to act as a substitute for the work requirement. Fortunately, Lieutenant-Governor Jane Swift, who replaced Governor Paul Cellucci, was persuaded by the business community to take a more enlightened approach. Acknowledging that a more educated citizenry is good for the state, welfare mothers in Massachusetts are now permitted to make up half of their work requirement by going to school.

In April 1997, the *New York Times* published a lengthy interview that reporter Jason De Parle held with sociologist Kathryn Eden, who had just published a book called *Making Ends Meet*. She reported that most women cheat on welfare. They have to. Welfare never provides enough money for rent and food. Hardships continued all during this welfare-to-work period. Eight in ten recipients had severe housing problems. One in six had recently been homeless. One-third had run out of food sometime in the last year. And conditions had not really improved for those who appeared to have moved up one step, to an entry-level job. In examining the budgets of 165 working mothers, Eden found them even more likely than those on welfare to be unable to pay their bills. Eden commented, "I thought they might be the same, but not worse."

Here are Eden's tallies: (1997) The typical welfare household spent $876 a month—$311 more than the average package of welfare and food stamps. That left the welfare mother to raise one-third of her income through off-the-book stratagems. These include donations from friends and family ($62), contributions from various fathers ($95), and earnings, mostly under the table ($128). About 8% acknowledged raising money from illegal activity, such as prostitution and drugs. Her final finding was that working mothers with comparable skills and education fared even worse than those on welfare. Ostensibly, work brought more money—42% more, or $1,243 a month. But work-related expenses like clothing, childcare, and transportation ate up virtually all the gain. In addition, 40% of the working mothers lacked health insurance while women on welfare received Medicaid.

The evaluations of this bold new no-welfare world continue. Wisconsin, first and most thorough in its work-to-welfare programs, says it spent a lot of money up front, but anticipates that it will begin saving money in three to five years. Oregon was not far behind Wisconsin in reducing its caseload. In November 1997, Oregon reported a 51% decline. Officials estimated that 75% of those left on the rolls in Oregon suffered from mental health problems that could interfere with a job. Half acknowledged drug or alcohol abuse and half said they had been sexually abused. (Compared to the general population, a disproportionatenumber of women on welfare report being sexually abused as children.) Forty-two percent lacked a high school education and 30% had criminal histories. Social workers call this group that gets left behind "the next challenging question to welfare reformers."

The political right says all women need is the threat of the loss of benefits and they will shape up, becoming breadwinners overnight. They will discover that they had the right work habits all along. The left says that's wrong. The women have to be trained to gain skills and the right work habits, and gently, slowly removed from welfare dependency, then they will discover how much they like working. The left is closer, but not close enough. The left does not acknowledge the need for close mentoring. New York University expert Lawrence Mead describes a particularly successful program in Kenosha County, Wisconsin. All recipients go through a spell of working part time before they get trained for anything. Then the training begins. Their program is extremely paternalistic. Case managers follow up on clients closely to be sure they get the help they need to participate but also to verify that they fulfill their assignments and do not drop out. No one is permitted to refuse this "inquisitorial" approach. It has a high success rate for keeping people on jobs.

Regrettably, this is an isolated example. Personalized casework was supposed to be a hallmark of this welfare-to-work bill, but surveys indicate that for the vast numbers of people involved, it never happened.

By the fortunate happenstance of a five-year period of economic boom, it was easier than anyone imagined to reduce welfare rolls. Using 1994 as the baseline year, a year during which the number of welfare recipients peaked at 14 million, by December 1997, the rolls had dropped by 27% to 11.25 million and were expected to continue to fall. The Council of Economic Advisers said that half of the decline stemmed from the nation's recent economic growth, citing the low unemployment rate of 4.6%. The General Accounting Office added (*New York Times*, June 3, 1999) that the test of the 1996 act will come when the next recession hits and there is no federal safety net for the first time in sixty years.

Where does our nation stand with regard to the poor in the year 2000? President Clinton was pleased to report at a news conference on April 11, 1999, that welfare caseloads had dropped to 7.6 million people, the lowest level since 1969. Experts believe that about half of those who leave welfare actually have jobs. The half of the welfare population that lost welfare and found no jobs has vanished as a statistic. They are worse off than before. One finds them in trailer parks and on soup lines, in homeless shelters and emergency rooms, but they have not surfaced as a discernible group. Federal and state health policy experts reported to the *New York Times* on April 12, 1999, that hundreds of thousands of low-income people nationwide have lost health-insurance coverage as an unintended consequence of the 1996 welfare law. The reason is that, in spite of the federal law to the contrary, administrators of the Medicaid programs discontinued coverage for those who left welfare to take jobs.

There remain 12.7% of Americans living below the official poverty line of $16,660 for a family of four, according to *The Economist* of September 30, 2000. Public policy can help the working poor enormously by making childcare more accessible, affordable, and of higher quality. Although the crisis in childcare that was predicted has not materialized, the quality of care remains a major concern. The February 4, 2000, *New York Times* reported that "About a million additional toddlers and preschoolers are in childcare because of changes in the welfare laws, but many are in low-quality care and are lagging in language and social development." One is tempted to ask if it really is necessary to have a woman at a menial job while her four-year-old is sitting in a room with twelve other children watching television for most of the day. And it's not clear that states will continue to spend so much of their own money on childcare. Subsidized childcare in 1998 cost the states $1.6 billion of their money and $3.5 billion in federal funds. This money helped only 10% of the children eligible.

As for jobs, public policy can assist the working poor by alleviating some of the transportation costs incurred as urban dwellers scramble to find a way to get to their jobs in the suburbs. There are two problems are highlighted by the fact that America's working poor live in straightened circumstances in the cities while job growth is in the suburbs. The first problem is in housing. Since the 1970s, the supply of low-income renters has risen by more than two-thirds, while the number of cheap rentals has fallen. This is partly because Congress drastically cut the amount of money appropriated for low-income housing in the 1990s and only began to restore it in the 1998 budget. Economists say that a family can live within its means if it spends 25% of its income for shelter. In reality, 60% of the income of the poor goes to shelter. Ironically, some of the drop in affordable housing can be attributed to successful slum-clearance programs. But even an increase in affordable housing would not help the working poor get to work. The working poor need subsidies for transportation costs within the city and affordable transportation from the city to the suburbs, where the jobs are.

There must also be a wage policy. The bitterest part of the job search is not finding it in a place that's hard to travel to, but what's available when it is found. Wages are typically low, and job loss and part-time work are common. A 1998 issue of *The Economist* reported that only 13% of poor adults had full-time jobs. The earliest surveys suggest that many who leave welfare for work still remain in poverty. A University of Wisconsin study reported that the annual earnings of new workers one year off welfare came to $7,700, a mere 59% of the $13,000 the government says a family of three needs to escape poverty. Therefore, getting off welfare has reduced their annual income by $400 and cost them their Medicaid card. As De Parle observed, "The journey from welfare to work is a story of running in place."

Jason de Parle filed his final report in December 1999. He said that after three years of tracking the nation's anti-welfare campaigns, what was most noteworthy about the lives of the poor was not change, but the long list of things that remained the same: violent neighborhoods, absent fathers, bare cupboards, epidemics of depression, the temptations of drugs, the threat to personal safety from street fights and guns. Every anxiety remained—worries about kids left alone while Mom was working, worries about getting the money for asthma medication, worries about abusive boyfriends. The job was just one more nuisance to deal with, and an exhausting one at that. The women did not understand that they were supposed to feel "pride" because they were working. They were just too tired. They would have given up their jobs in a minute—less than a minute.

CHAPTER EIGHT

CHILDREN'S WELFARE, CHILDREN'S RIGHTS

1960–2000

CHAPTER EIGHT

Children's Welfare, Children's Rights

1960–2000

Introduction

How a nation cares for its poor, and particularly its poor children, is an important marker of how civilized and humane that nation is. The record for the United States is uneven. Since children were not regarded as human beings with "rights" for the first three hundred years of our history, little ink needs to be spilled discussing early "rights." The first children recognized as having "rights" were suffering either from abuse at the hands of a caretaker (Mary Ellen, 1874, New York Court) or from abuse at the hands of a judicial court (the child coal thief in Judge Ben Lindsay's Denver Court, 1900). But over time, accelerating in the last thirty-five years, "children's rights" has grown to include the right to be free of abuse, the right to a safe and nurturing environment, and the right to fair treatment in court.

Children's Welfare Policy

The findings on child abuse published by Dr. Henry C. Kempe in 1962 mark the beginning of the nation's understanding of child abuse. Dr. Kempe and five colleagues had convened to review fifteen years of findings on children who were treated for multiple bruises or occasional fractures that parents could not explain. They exposed a devastating secret. Their findings, reported in the *Journal of the American Medical Association*, revealed that significant numbers of parents and caretakers battered their children, even to death. The Battered Child Syndrome, as it was called, describes a pattern of child abuse resulting in certain clinical conditions and establishes a medical and psychiatric model of the causes of child abuse. It marked the development of child abuse as a distinct academic subject. The article urged physicians to adopt a higher level of suspicion and to take a more aggressive role in preventing future harm to the child. This report is generally regarded as one of the most significant events leading to professional and public awareness of the magnitude of child abuse and neglect in the nation and throughout the world. In response to the article, Congress passed a law that required that cases of abuse be reported.

There was some fear that class bias would creep into the reports, and that there were no guidelines as to what was to be reported and to whom. The answer to both of these difficulties lay in "reporting laws." Thus, within a few years of the report, forty-nine states had statutes defining "mandated reporters" and guidelines as to what constituted physical abuse. Mandated reporters are those childcare professionals who are *legally required* to report suspected cases of child abuse. In Massachusetts, mandated reporters include doctors, all other hospital personnel, mental-health professionals (including drug and alcohol counselors), emergency medical technicians, firefighters, schoolteachers, and daycare workers. The Massachusetts statute, like most of the other states, *levies criminal sanctions for failure to report*. The reporter is provided with immunity from either civil or criminal liability for making the report. Physicians, the most likely childcare workers to see abuse, are granted a waiver from their confidentiality restraints. After a report is made to the Department of Social Services (henceforth DSS or the department), DSS investigates. If the second report substantiates a finding of abuse, the case becomes a child protection case in a juvenile or a family court. To qualify to receive federal money, a jurisdiction must appoint a *guardian ad litem* for the children. In the years following the initial legislation, Massachusetts added two more provisions to its Child Abuse Reporting Law. It mandated that DSS notify the district attorney of severe physical or sexual abuse. That notification, in turn, triggers the response of a multi-disciplinary team that includes a DSS worker and a representative of the district attorney's office. They examine each case referred by DSS to the district attorney and determine whether the case should be criminally prosecuted.

Between the time that social service agencies first understood the crime called "child abuse" and the present, the number of reported and substantiated cases has grown to a number that no one anticipated. In 1990, the U.S. Advisory Board on Child Abuse and Neglect concluded that, "The scope of the problem of child maltreatment is so enormous and serious, and the failure of the system designed to deal with the problem so catastrophic, that the crises has reached a national emergency."

And the number kept growing. Between 1990 and 1996, more than three million reports alleging abuse or neglect were filed annually. Forty percent, or 1.2 million, were substantiated. Included in that number were 160,000 cases of serious injury and 2,000 deaths. Findings of abuse lead to the removal of children from their homes. In 2000, 550,000 children were in foster care in the United States. From the mid-1980s to the late 1990s, the number of children removed from their homes increased 74%; the length of time children remained in care and their rate of re-entry into care also rose.

A survey of Massachusetts in 1997 found 13,000 children in foster care in 6,500 homes. In the next three years, the Massachusetts Department of Social

Services experienced a daily increase of twenty children entering its child-protection system. The increase of the children needing placement is said to be a consequence of two phenomena of the nineties. The first is the explosion of drug addiction. In 1990 the *Boston Globe* reported the rise of cocaine use as a factor in 59% of all supported Department of Social Service investigations. The second is the intensification of urban poverty. As previously discussed, child-welfare statisticians correlate a 10% rise in substantiated abuse cases in Massachusetts over the three-year period since the 1997 Welfare Reform Bill went into effect.

When the Department of Social Services removes a child from home, they must then place the child somewhere. Usually the placement is with a relative ("kinship care") or with a foster home approved by DSS ("stranger care"). The supply of non-family foster homes is steadily dwindling. There are several reasons for this. As more women need to contribute to the family coffers, work outside the home usurps work inside the home.[10] The children coming into care tend to be more emotionally damaged and more difficult to manage than they were in previous years. Finally, social service agencies themselves are sometimes an obstacle to finding and maintaining good foster homes. For example, they will dismiss a foster home because the bedroom intended for the child does not have the required square footage. A policy that created a significant drop in the number of kinship placements has been alluded to previously: the blind enforcement of a law designed to disqualify any home where a family member has a criminal record, even a trivial one such as a twenty-year-old charge of welfare fraud. One reads of this policy and thinks, "That makes

---

[10] Massachusetts foster families receive $14.95 a day for children ages 0-5, $15.47 a day for children ages 6-12, $17.16 for children ages 13-18, and a quarterly clothing allowance. They are currently being asked to raise a child on $5,000 a year. The best foster parents probably lose money rather than profit. The cost to the state is 4 million a year.

sense. Who would advocate putting a child in a home where another resident has a criminal record?" However, the agency is too short on placements, especially ones where the child knows the family and is comfortable. Acknowledging this, the Massachusetts legislature had obligated the department to modify this policy.

The department wants the children to be well cared for, but it does not want and will not support an affectionate bond between a foster parent and foster child. The department does this because it knows the difficulties that will ensue when the court decides to return the children to the custody of their parents. However, after a foster family experiences a few painful episodes—for example, an unexpected court order followed by an abrupt removal of a foster child—the family is unlikely to take more children. Until a change in the law in 1997, the system trivialized the feelings of foster families by refusing them the right to address the court. This refusal to acknowledge that they cared, that they had something important to say about the disposition of the case, was traumatizing. Since the new federal law came into effect, foster parents, preadoptive parents, and relatives providing care have had the right to receive notice of court proceedings and an opportunity to be heard. But they still do not have an automatic right to counsel, and the judge can exclude them from the hearing if he or she so chooses. That the fate of a child one has loved and cared for is being decided by those who know her less well, or not at all, engenders great bitterness. This presents DSS and the courts with a terrible conflict: they want to respect parents' legal rights, respect an emotional attachment between foster parent and child, and do what's best for the child. It is clear, however, that if DSS is going to recruit more quality placements, it must work with the courts to allow those foster parents who have had children for an extended period of time ("extended" to be defined by the law) full participation at hearings that determine the disposition of the child.

Foster care has never been well managed. Even before the numbers exploded and overwhelmed the social service agencies, too little attention was paid to the quality of foster care and the psychological well being of the child in placement. There are about 130,000 licensed foster families in the United States. The quality of foster care ranges from wonderful, as in the cases of specially-trained foster mothers handling severely medically-impaired children, to horrendous, such as the four-year experience of daily sexual abuse inflicted by the natural son of a foster mother, a case which is detailed in Chapter Ten. In between, there is a great deal of benign custodial care. The child is clothed and fed, has his schoolwork checked and his medical appointments kept—all things that were not part of his life before—but he receives no genuine nurturing. Given the shortage of placements, the child will probably be placed in a home that has more than the department's limit of three foster children per family. Moreover, the child might be placed in a home where the language spoken is not his own, will be moved once or twice if better openings become available, and, although this is against department policy, will not be placed with siblings due to space limitations. In 1998, in response to the frequency with which separated siblings could not see each other, the Massachusetts legislature passed a law stating that siblings separated in foster care should have access to and visitation rights with their siblings whenever reasonable and practical. This is a fine sentiment, but precedent suggests there is simply no way, with current resources, to implement it fully.

Consider this foster child for a moment. She is eight years old. She has already suffered trauma, a tear in the thin fabric woven between her and her parents. Even if she is being rescued from assault, the strange new home will produce more gloom and fear. She has to adapt to new rules and regulations, different styles of cooking, and adjust to a new set of relationships with other foster children, who, traumatized like herself, may be aggressive or violent. She may have to do this once or twice more in the course of her placement. She may encounter another abusive adult. She begins to understand that there is no security and no predictable future. Her ability to bond with an adult may wither, along with trust, optimism, and self-confidence. She's anxious and hurt and may begin a pattern of misbehavior. A host of questions confront her. Can she see her mother again? When? Who will take care of her mother? Many children in dysfunctional families believe that they are the caretakers for their parents. Who will take care of her siblings, or conversely, who will take care of her, now that the brother she has relied on is in a different placement? The success of the social worker's duty to arrange sibling visits depends entirely on the size of her caseload, the distances she has to drive to get the siblings together, and her willingness to set aside a mountain of paperwork to spend an afternoon trying to arrange a sibling visit. What if there are two cases that need sibling visits? Three?

The sibling problem is especially vexing. Siblings in different placements have different experiences. Because of the different ages and personalities in a sibling group, one or two of the siblings may be considered for adoption by a foster family, but the others not. While Massachusetts works very hard to get adoptions for its permanently placed children, department policy is that siblings may not be adopted separately—they must be adopted together or not at all. This creates a painful dilemma. The policy is based on the belief that if the sibling group is permanently split apart the children are further traumatized. However, large sibling groups usually have a range of ages, from toddler to adolescent. An adolescent is viewed as essentially unadoptable. Is it fair to keep a toddler in foster care all of his life because nobody wants to adopt his diffi-cult thirteen-year-old brother? Further, it's possible his thirteen-year-old brother has abused him and should never be placed with him. The depart-ment has struggled with this problem, and has gone both ways, both permit-ting and denying adoption of a part-sibling group.

Our eight-year-old's problems are not over. She has never attended school with any regularity and is increasingly unable to keep up. She is getting dis-couraged, embarrassed by never knowing the right answers; when she's in school she masks her despair by acting out, and receives various punishments. Now, after her removal from her home, she is placed in a new school. But this will not occur immediately. First, her school records have to be sent to the new school and a new bus route has to be planned. In Boston, this takes about two weeks. What happens if this young person is moved *twice* in one school year, and in spite of efforts to the contrary, has to change school again? A recent study in California indicated that a foster child could expect to attend an aver-age of nine or ten schools by the age of eighteen. The reader is correctly seeing early school dropout writ large on this child's future. This will be accompa-nied by anger, depression, and further loss of self-esteem. In all probability, we are witnessing the development of a future teen-age welfare mother, or, if we are talking about a young boy, a pre-teen participant in the kind of small crime that leads to bigger crime.

Contributing to her anxiety is her uncertain future: will she ever be reunited with her family, and if not, where will she live? When will she know the answer to this? One of the cruelest, most destructive habits of social serv-ice agencies and courts has been to allow children in foster care to languish year after year, their case never brought into court for a hearing, their fate never determined, permanency never achieved.

This lack of a permanent plan is called "foster-care drift;" it afflicts more than 50% of the children in foster care in the United States. The federal government, under the prodding of the Child Welfare League and the Children's Defense Fund, crafted several pieces of helpful legislation. In 1980, in 1985, and again in 1993 the government provided money to the states to fund family preservation projects. If the family could be preserved, the children would not have to be placed in foster care.

The government and childcare agencies were acting on the received wisdom of the day, which was to maintain families, not separate them. The book behind these policy decisions was *In the Best Interests of the Child.* Like John Bowlby before them, the authors, child psychologists Joseph Goldstein, Anna Freud, and Albert Solnit argued that a child's healthy development depends on a stable *psychological* parent. They found foster care unsatisfactory because of its inherent lack of permanence. Goldstein et al defined a psychological parent as one who has day-to-day interaction, companionship, and shared experiences with the child. The role could be filled by almost anyone, but the person must be there consistently with the child. They said that foster mothers, either by nature or by instruction from the Department of Social Services (recall the preceding discussion), did not adequately bond with their foster children; the children under their care did not form the critical attachment to an adult caretaker. Therefore, Goldstein and his fellow authors recommended that placement decisions be determined by the child's need for continuity.

The book was first published in 1973. Its popularity was limited at first, but over time its tenets became a kind of childcare creed. Legislatures began to fund programs that put homemaker helpers, parenting advisors, and similar personnel into homes so that uninformed or overstressed parentscould get the help they needed to maintain the family unit and prevent their children from being removed from their homes.

These programs, if they were to succeed, needed carefully trained, well-paid workers, workers who were willing to commit substantial hours for considerable periods of time. Research demonstrated that parents could learn new attitudes if they had a supportive relationship with the right mentor. But these programs were never adequately funded, and the amount of in-home assistance was no match for the growing population of seriously drug-addicted mothers and their badly-neglected offspring. The children paid a heavy price for this policy. Far too often, they were maintained in a home from which they should have been removed

Since the policy to keep families together at all costs was undermined by the obvious failures of the policy to keep the child's needs foremost, in 1997 Congress reevaluated previous legislation. With the Adoption and Safe Families Act (ASFA), federal money was now allocated to programs that hastened adoption. The new law took money out of homemaking services and put it into adoption services. Adoption, instead of family reunification, was favored.

Under the current law, social service agencies have twelve or fifteen months, depending on the circumstances, to provide the court with a permanent plan for the child. (A permanent plan means that DSS decides that the children will be either re-unified with their parents, or freed for adoption.) The state will not receive federal funds if it does not comply with this requirement. It is the most successful assault on foster-care drift to date. In Massachusetts, the department has used the federal money to enlarge its adoption division. Despite the addition of new children to the foster-care roster every day, the department has reduced the number of children suspended in foster care from

13,000 in 1997 to 9,000 in 2000. However, in spite of strenuous efforts, the waiting period between when a child is freed for adoption and when the adoption is completed is three years, reduced from the former five years. This is still too long. And merely shortening the waiting time for adoption leaves other foster care problems unaddressed. Many of the children will still experience the cycle of removal, return, and removal. Many will still be placed in more than one foster home, and some of the foster homes will further traumatize them. And some of the children, although freed for adoption, will be in the age group from whom there are very few adoptions.

The system has additional flaws. Most noticeable is the time-frame provision. The twelve or fifteen month period means that the parent has this period of time in which to satisfy the department's requirements for reunification. These requirements are specified in a service plan. If the parent cannot comply with the social services plan's requirements for reasons that are beyond her control, the time limit can be extended. An examination of the drug rehabilitation requirement illustrates the problem. Completing a drug rehabilitation program is often a part of the department's service plan. The mother must be fully compliant before she can recover her children. If spaces are not available, the clock can't start running on her allotted twelve months. Also, there are constant interruptions with court calendars causing delays in court hearing dates. Again, the twelve-month period has to be extended, and again, it is beyond the client's control.

The Congressionally mandated time standards work in favor of the children needing permanent placement outside the home and against those parents who need more time to regain custody. Their rights will be discussed in Chapter Nine.

Alternatives for children who will not be re-united with biological parents

Fortunately, there have been a series of developments that mitigate the harshness of the foster-care/adoption paradigm of the past. Short of outright adoption, social service agencies and courts offer the option of legal guardianship. Legal guardianship is an ill-defined condition that stops just short of adoption. While it does not satisfy a child's need for closure, it makes it more difficult for a biological parent to sue for return of custody. It's the solution most often used when a parent is losing custody of a child to the custody of her own sibling. In a situation fraught with such family tension, it's best to avoid a termination-of-rights trial and allow a legal guardianship.

Long-term residence in a treatment center is another placement option. There are a certain number of abused children whose personalities have disintegrated, and therefore cannot be maintained in a private residence. They are a threat to either themselves or others. In addition to the behavior and attachment disorders common to children who have been abused and moved around a lot, some children have neurological problems stemming from having been exposed *in utero* to crack cocaine or excessive amounts of alcohol. Another source of neurological problems is the lead paint that remains, illegally, on the walls of ghetto apartments. It is estimated that, nationwide, about 16%, or 65,000, children removed from their biological homes are emotionally disturbed and in need of therapy. They are sent either to the long term residences mentioned above, or shorter term group homes. In both cases in Massachusetts the facilities are staffed with partially trained residence counselors and fully trained professional therapists.

The success of this kind of placement is uneven and unpredictable. The children are somewhat helped if their families visit and participate in the "family therapy" session. But often there is no family. As for progress in becoming a human being whose behavior is more acceptable, in spite of hours and hours of therapy and behavior modification, anti-psychotic drugs (for which a court order is required), and every tool that counselors can devise, nothing seems to help as much as simply getting older. Some residents enter at age eight and leave at age eighteen. Gradually, over the years, they learn a certain degree of insight and self-control. Will it last outside the residential setting? Very little solid research is available on whether institutionalizing children does them any lasting good. Indeed, experts disagree widely about the criteria of success, let alone to what extent success is achieved.

In 1994, the cost for institutional care was about $40,000 per child per year. As one might anticipate, questions arise about a program with such a high price tag, the success or failure of which is random and not quantifiable. But there is one inescapable reality: where there is no family, there must be an institution. The institution can be an almshouse, an orphanage, a Charles Loring Brace orphan train, a residential treatment center, or a small parent-run unit of troubled children. Leaving troubled children to their own devices is not acceptable.

Adoption is another choice society offers for children who cannot live with their parents. Children become available for adoption if their parents voluntarily relinquish them or if the court terminates parental rights. An estimated 130,000 children are adopted each year. About half are adopted by relatives, and between 15 and 20% are adopted by their foster family. There is no reliable data on other types of adoption.

The federal government, as previously noted, has been instrumental in freeing more children for adoption in the early stages of placement. It has encouraged foster parents to adopt children with special needs by providing financial assistance to help defray medical costs. It encouraged color-blind adoptions. The states also get money for each adoption of a child who is difficult place (such as an older child or a child with a physical, mental, or emotional disability).

Throughout this century, especially in last thirty years, trials for the termination of parental rights have been a source of conflict and heartache. The trial was the only way for parents to contest the agency's decision. The trial was brutally punishing to parents because, in order to be persuasive to the judge, the department had to prove that a parent was unfit to keep her child. The parent sat through a trial in which her mothering and her personality were severely criticized, her failures exposed in vividly painful language. It was punishing to children because trials take time, sometimes up to two years (due to delays, continuances, and so forth). For the entire duration of the trial, the child did not know whether he would be ordered to return to his parents, whom he may have left years earlier. Until the trial was over and a possible appeal by the parent resolved, the child could not be freed for adoption.

Enlightened social workers and attorneys have introduced new procedures to eliminate the pain of an adoption trial. The first new procedure is Permanency Mediation. This is a form of specialized alternative dispute resolution that uses a clinically trained mediator to facilitate a child-centered, family-focused approach to permanency planning. The process brings together, in one room, at one time, parents, relatives, professionals and community members to develop a permanency plan rooted in the children's best interest. In cases where reunification is not possible, birth parents and adopting parents are given the responsibility for cooperatively designing a plan for their child's future. By the time the process is completed, every participant thinks that this *is* the best plan for the children and will support it. If an agreement cannot be reached, the family and the social service agency will then proceed to a standard termination trial.

Massachusetts has begun its own Permanency Mediation Program and Family Consultation Team. The mediation offered is the standard mediation involving just the parties to the conflict and the mediator. Since its inception in 1967, it has brought sixty-five cases to successful completion, representing approximately half of the cases it has undertaken. Mary Le Beau, the director of the Permanency Mediation Program, says that the average child in foster care waits three and a half years between the time DSS files a petition to terminate parental rights and the moment that the final court proceeding ends. With permanency mediation, the time is shortened to five months. The goal is to bring the program to every court in the Commonwealth. This goal looks reachable; the juvenile-court justices are increasingly supportive and the state legislature has generously funded the project. Only the Department of Social Services (DSS) stubbornly refuses to employ it.

The second innovation to soften the pain of court-ordered surrendering of one's children is open adoptions. Before 1980, Massachusetts followed social agencies' usual habits: DSS chose the adopting parents, and the birth parents received little information about the adopting couple. Now, there is a movement to offer much broader, more open, and more direct exchange of information between birth parents and adoptive parents throughout the process. If a working relationship has been established during the foster-care period, and the adoptive mother feels comfortable with this, an open adoption agreement can be concluded with varying degrees of future contact, for example, yearly pictures or visits. The Massachusetts version of the Federal Safe Families Act explicitly provides for post-adoptive contact agreements. Much of the program's success rests on the personalities and interaction of the foster mother and the biological mother. They have to respect each other, and they have to behave in such a way that the child knows that his adoptive mother is his for keeps. The experiment of open adoption has to be studied over a longer period of time before it can be given a passing or a failing grade. Massachusetts' courts have given conflicting signals with regard to their approval. But on the whole it is a promising development, since it helps to avoid a bruising, lengthy termination trial.

A survey of the options reveals a gaping hole. Very young children need something that is not available: the small group home. Nineteenth-century Germany created small, two-parent "family" units of no more than six children. The two-parent unit recreated an artificial family with rules, meal times, school reports, and other aspects of family life. Perhaps, at some point, America could experiment with this.

Concluding this mixed review of the circumstances of American children today, one is still looking at poverty. One in five American children lives in poverty. The figure has not changed over the past decade and is twice as high as those of the industrialized nations of Europe. As Marian Wright Edleman, Director of the Children's Defense Fund, has observed, America is first in its number of millionaires and billionaires, first in defense expenditures, first in the size of its national GNP, and seventeenth in its expenditures on programs that would lift children out of poverty.

Before he left office, Ronald Reagan appointed a bipartisan body of thirty-four members to study children's lives. In 1991, it issued a report called "Beyond Rhetoric," which exposed the consequences of poverty. One quarter of pregnant women in the nation received prenatal care too late or not at all, which resulted in an exceptionally high rate of premature births, underweight infants, and infant deaths. Many preschool children who were examined in emergency rooms needed treatment for malnourishment, lead poisoning, whooping cough, and improperly handled asthma. About half of the preschool children were not immunized against routine childhood diseases. Since the time the report was issued, Congress has passed a law mandating healthcare coverage for all poor children. But mothers are not informed about the program and not given help in filling out the complex application form. Too few avail themselves of this new law.

School dropout rates at the time of the report are simply scandalous for a highly industrialized country. The proportion of children leaving school before graduation has held steady at 13% for years, and that figure does not reflect the number who graduate and are actually illiterate. One study in 1992 said that half the seventeen-year-old graduates could not read or understand English, and that 41% could not work with numbers beyond the four basic calculations.

Juvenile Law

Delinquency and the Juvenile Court

Juvenile courts in Massachusetts primarily deal with two different assign-ments. One assignment, akin to criminal law, is to handle youths brought before it on delinquency charges, such as petty theft or property destruction. The other assignment is to attend to the care-and-protection petitions filed on behalf of children by the Department of Social Services. This is known as the "dependency court." This chapter addresses the delinquency court. Chapter nine discusses the dependency court.

As has been noted, observers of the juvenile court in the early 1960s were troubled by the seeming absence of procedural rights and the absolute author-ity granted to the judge. They accused the judiciary of abusing its powers under the authority granted to it by the centuries-old doctrine of *parens patriae,* the court acting in place of the parent. In large part, the juvenile courts of the first six decades of the twentieth century operated without any one checking on them. Without oversight of some sort, juveniles could not be guaranteed fair treatment in court.

The casual absence of procedural guarantees came to an end with two United States Supreme Court cases. In *Kent v. United States,* 1966, the initial trial court had not permitted a juvenile, Morris A. Kent, either a lawyer or a real hearing. In two quick, irregular courtroom procedures the presiding judge sentenced Morris Kent to ninety years in prison for a series of house break-ins. U.S. Supreme Court Justice Justice Abe Fortas, writing a majority opinion that reversed the lower court's order, said,

> The right to representation is not a formality. It is not a grudging gesture to a ritualistic requirement. It is of the essence of justice.

> Appointment of counsel without affording an opportunity for a hearing on a critically important decision is tantamount to denial of counsel, and it was error to fail to grant a hearing. The hearing must measure up to the essentials of due process and fair treatment. Counsel must be afforded access to records requested.

Kent set the precedent for a case in the next Supreme Court term that locked in due process rights for juveniles all over the country. *In Re Gault* struck the final blow to a court's *parens patriae* authority.

On June 5, 1964, Gerald Gault, age fifteen, was committed to the Arizona State Industrial Training School until he reached adult status—a term of six years. What was his crime? A few weeks earlier, he and a friend had telephoned a woman and made mildly lewd remarks to her. Although the Court's written opinion in the *Gault* does not tell us what the lewd remarks were, the Court stated that "it will suffice for purposes of this opinion to say that the remarks or questions put to her were of the irritatingly offensive, adolescent sex variety." If an adult had been convicted of the same crime, the penalty would have been a fine of $5 to $50 and no more than two months in jail.

Neither Gerald Gault nor his parents were represented by counsel at either of the two hearings that were held, and no one told them they had the right to counsel. The judge questioned Gerald at both hearings but did not tell him he had the right to refuse to answer questions. The woman making the complaint never appeared in the courtroom. No record was kept of what transpired at either hearing. Nonetheless, Gerald was committed to the state industrial school for six years.

His parents sued, claiming that their son's procedural rights had been violated. Their appeal reached the Supreme Court in January 1967. On May 15, 1967, Justice Abe Fortas wrote the decision for an 8-1 Court. He reviewed the procedural history of the case and the historical shortcomings of the juvenile court process. In his opinion, the belief that the juvenile court could best care for juvenile defendants without the distraction of due process was a myth, and that due process, not benevolent intentions, produced justice. He continued his opinion,

> Under our Constitution, the condition of being a boy does not justify a kangaroo Court...The essential difference between Gerald's case and a normal criminal case is that safeguards available to adults were discarded in Gerald's case. The summary procedure as well as the long commitment was possible because Gerald was fifteen years of age instead of over eighteen.

> If Gerald had been over eighteen, he would have not been subject to juvenile court proceedings. For the particular offense immediately involved, the maximum punishment would have been a fine of $5 to $50, or imprisonment in jail for not more than two months...neither the Fourteenth Amendment nor the Bill of Rights is for adults alone.

The indicting pen of Abe Fortas resurrected the long-somnolent interest in children's legal rights. The seventies yielded some progress, in the form of the American Bar Association's carefully crafted "Juvenile Justice Standards" (guidelines to help judges deliver uniform judgments in their courts) and the 1974 Juvenile Justice and Delinquency Prevention Act (JJDP). The reforms introduced by this act bore a striking similarity in words and goals to reforms of earlier eras that were abandoned before they began. These reforms will sound familiar: juveniles arrested for "juvenile crimes" like truancy, running away, or stubborn behavior could not be placed in secure detention facilities with adult criminals. These *status* offenses[11] were not to be considered criminal acts. Juveniles found guilty in these cases were to be

---

[11] A status offense is an offense that only a juvenile can commit, like being absent from school.

diverted into rehabilitative programs in the community and monitored by a probation officer. Due process in all juvenile proceedings, beginning with the initial hearing, was to be guaranteed.

In 1980, a survey of juvenile detention procedures revealed that juveniles were still being locked up with adults, still routinely physically and sexually abused in these facilities. Therefore, in 1980 the law was amended to establish, among other things, a strict five-year deadline for the removal of juveniles from adult lock-up in every jurisdiction in the country.

Unfortunately, during the eighties serious juvenile crime was increasing. Americans attributed this perceived rise in crime to the leniency with which offenders were treated. In 1982, the Reagan Administration tried to dismantle the Office of Juvenile Justice by eliminating its budget. Congress refused to comply and refunded it through 1984. Reagan then appointed Alfred Regnery as Office Administrator. Regnery was opposed to all programs that did not punish delinquents and therefore redirected the money to programs that emphasized prosecution and jailing of juvenile delinquents. But his program re-direction was modest compared to what came next.

The decade of the 1990s brought enormous wrath down on the heads of juveniles under eighteen. It is they who appeared to be bearing the brunt of the public anger about crime, drugs, violence, and an atomized urban society. Sweeping changes in public policy have resulted from this universal crackdown on juvenile crime committed by young people at increasingly younger ages. The first of these new statutes makes it easier to transfer juvenile offenders from the juvenile-justice system to the adult criminal-justice system. Since 1996, forty-nine of the fifty states have changed their laws to allow more children to be tried as adults. The Massachusetts law is typical. In 1996, under the Juvenile Justice Reform Act, the decision as to whether a juvenile should be tried as an adult was taken out of the hands of judges, where it had been for almost 100 years, and put into the hands of the district attorney. The district attorney, acting as prosecutor for the state, may request a transfer hearing for a child fourteen years or older who has allegedly committed an offense for which an adult could be sent to a state prison. The prosecutor must establish that the child is a threat to himself or others, and that he is not amenable to rehabilitation within the juvenile justice system. (Massachusetts General Laws, Chapter 119, § 61).

Nationwide, transfer is being used not only to send violent offenders to adult court. *Property and public disorder offenses now make up the largest proportion of juvenile transfer cases.* In March 2000, the United States Department of Justice released a study showing that between 1985 and 1997, the number of defendants under eighteen sentenced to long prison terms in adult prisons doubled. Four states—New York, Illinois, North Carolina, and Florida—have over 400 children under the age of eighteen committed to adult prisons. Nearly half the states have no minimum age requirement, and one (Kansas) has a minimum age of ten. In addition to the doubling of juvenile offenders in adult facilities, the number of juveniles locked up in cells with adult criminals while awaiting trial or serving short terms has more than quadrupled. It is distressing to see fifty years of progress toward a more enlightened view of juvenile law wiped out in half a decade. According to research published by the *Juvenile and Family Court Journal*, incarceration with adults increases the likelihood that juveniles will commit suicide or become victims of rape, assault, and murder. The concept of rehabilitation is distant memory.

The second of the new statutes has had a dramatic impact on sentencing practices. These included the imposition of mandatory minimum sentences, permission for judges to send juveniles to adult prisons rather than juvenile detention centers, and allowing the judge, if he so chooses, to add an adult sentence to a juvenile court sentence once the juvenile becomes an adult.

The retributive mode continues through the present. *Although juvenile crime rates have been dropping for the last five years,* legislatures are mandating longer sentences and governors are spending money to expand detention facilities.

The greatest cause for concern among juvenile-justice advocates is the steady increase in death-penalty sentences for teens. Twenty-three of the thirty-eight states that allow the death penalty permit the execution of juvenile offenders, some as young as sixteen. Lest Americans question this practice on constitutional grounds, the Supreme Court assured the nation in a 1988 decision that, in the words of Justice Antonin Scalia, since there was no national consensus against the death penalty for youths under sixteen, it could not be described as cruel and unusual punishment and was, therefore, consistent with the Constitution.

English common law used seven as the age above which a child should understand the difference between right and wrong, and fourteen as the age above which a child had "criminal culpability," that is, could understand the consequences of his actions. In the twentieth century, the United States developed a more sophisticated understanding of teenage behavior. Research indicated that a young teen does not yet have a fully formed, dependable moral code, is still struggling with impulse control, and is profoundly unable to understand the consequences of his behavior. Until the 1980s, laws on juvenile crime and rehabilitation reflected these insights. The nation strove to base the juvenile justice system on rehabilitation.

This goal was accepted as a policy because citizens were persuaded that young people were both cognitively and morally undeveloped, and that their malleability made them susceptible to moral and social rehabilitation.

Moreover, modern-day Americans believe that they have abandoned the Puritan fathers' conviction that every child is born innately evil. We transformed the "born bad" belief into the "can be taught" belief. Briefly in the nineteenth century, but more pronounced in the twentieth, we came to understand that a child, a teenager, and an adult represent three distinct stages of life, each with its own set of behaviors and perceptions. Each stage is marked by distinct perceptions of acceptable and unacceptable behavior. This point of view was regarded as enlightened. It was one of the ways one could tell a civilized country from a less educated one But again, two Supreme Court Justices, Antonin Scalia and William Rehnquist, held the opinion that there was no developmental difference between a ten-year-old and a thirty-year-old, and that psychiatric evidence in a juvenile's trial was irrelevant because it was based on a discredited science.

Where are we now? Since the advent of the new laws allowing juveniles to be transferred to adult courts, thirteen men have been executed for crimes committed when they were juveniles. In January 2000, seventy more awaited execution. Amnesty International said this number exceeds the total in all other countries in the world. Only five other nations allow capital punishment for juveniles found guilty of murder: Iran, Nigeria, Pakistan, Saudi Arabia, and Yemen.

This brave new world was given a spin in Michigan in 1997 when, months before Michigan abolished age limits for juveniles, an eleven-year-old shot and killed an eighteen-year-old. After two years of detention, he was tried in adult court and found guilty. At the sentencing phase of his trial (he was now fourteen), the prosecutor and politicians pressed for the maximum sentence. The judge sentenced him to seven years in a juvenile detention center, after which he would be released. In response to the fury this "leniency" evoked, the judge said,

The legislature's response to juvenile crime is a very short-sighted solution. If we put more kids into a failed system, though we may house them where they cannot do any damage for a period of time, we should not be surprised when they emerge as more dangerous and hardened criminals. Instead of spending more money building more prisons, we should be spending money preventing crime and rehabilitating the youthful criminal. One of the strengths of the juvenile court system is that it actually works.

Juvenile offenders are further threatened by the continuing hostility of juvenile court judges to the procedural guarantees laid down by *Gault*. A 1994 survey of 100 juvenile court judges, lawyers, and probation officers revealed that nearly half the juvenile court judges described a courtroom in which the juvenile defendants could not get a fair trial. The most egregious failure was the right to competent representation. Numerous studies across the nation show a large percentage of juveniles waiving their right to counsel. Without a lawyer present, procedural due process is ignored, the defendant has no effective way of answering the charges before him, and cannot effectively argue for an alternative disposition to a sentence in juvenile detention.

Even when juveniles do have lawyers to represent them, the quality of the advocacy is too often deplorable. One New York study concluded that only 4% of the lawyers in juvenile court provided effective assistance. An American Bar Association study indicated that most juvenile defenders' caseloads are too large to allow time for genuine attention to each case. They do not even have time to meet with their clients before a hearing. Furthermore, half the juvenile lawyers surveyed had no training in the representation of juveniles. The overall atmosphere of the juvenile court, or what the study termed "courthouse culture," discouraged aggressive advocacy on the part of juvenile defenders. The study concluded that no one was taking these court proceedings seriously.

Thirty years after *Gault*, a juvenile in a juvenile court was still at the mercy of one arbitrary judge.

In spite of all the evidence to the contrary, juvenile court experts still believe that a one-judge court is more likely to render a fair verdict than a jury trial. In 1971, when the Supreme Court ruled that the constitution did not require jury trials in juvenile court, court reformers were in despair. But others argued that juries were inherently ill disposed toward juvenile offenders, and that, therefore, a trained, competent judge was the best choice. A trained, competent judge combined with trained legal counsel, counsel that is prepared to represent the juvenile from the time of the detention hearing through to the trial, prepared to take the time to interview witnesses and take depositions, would go a long way toward bringing justice to the juvenile court. Court reformers, however have another, better idea: family courts. These courts will be examined in Chapter Nine.

CHAPTER NINE

PARENTAL RIGHTS, FAMILY COURTS

1960–2000

CHAPTER NINE

Parental Rights, Family Courts

1960–2000

Parental Rights

Anglo-Saxons had a "family law policy." It was "A man's home is his castle." It meant that the government (the king) should stay out. It did not prevent the king from entering the home to order all young men into uniform for a war, but it prevented any one from interfering if a man beat his wife and children.

On this side of the Atlantic, the concept that the family was immune to outside interference slowly eroded among the earliest colonists. The Puritans felt duty-bound to remove children from homes where the parents were failing in their duty to instill Christian morals. By the decades after the Civil War, government-sanctioned private organizations worked to remove children from abusive parents, but there was no large-scale government policy to do so. In 1874, the Supreme Court of North Carolina ruled that under certain circumstances the curtain normally drawn over domestic life had to be lifted to expose a man's violent behavior toward his wife. This important first step in reducing family violence was not widely imitated.

The twentieth century substituted "family integrity" for the Anglo-Saxon credo, but the basic concept remained the same. However, as we examine America in the second half of the twentieth century, we see that the growing awareness of children's needs and rights has an immediate impact on parents' rights. Sometimes the two rights work in tandem; sometimes they work in opposition. The battleground for this conflict is a division of the juvenile court, the *dependency court*, where petitions for "care and protection" are heard for alleged cases of "abuse and neglect."

The notion that children are merely their parents' chattel was ostensibly discarded from our law long ago. The vision of today's family might be characterized as a social unit in which the minor child has certain basic rights, although the custodial parents retain governing powers throughout the child's minority. In modern times, parental "governing powers" have been steadily reduced. As we have seen, parental rule is subject to state scrutiny, under which an incompetent or harmful parent can be stripped of all or part of these governing powers. Although the government has this right, and exercises it with the approval of the citizenry, the citizenry utters a collective gasp. It is often difficult for ordinary men and women to reconcile the long-cherished belief that a family occupies a private space free from the intrusion of the world with the awareness that within that space some children are being starved, burned, beaten, and killed, and therefore must be taken away.

The conflict between parental rights and children's rights boils down to a definition of the phrase "best interests of the child." "Best interests," like "human nature," is a concept that eludes precise definition. For our purposes, "best interests" is defined as a child's need for emotional nurturance and physical safety. These needs sometimes collide with a parent's rights to custody. The conflict has been the subject of confused policy and much litigation. Currently, U.S. policy and the law state that "best interests" supersede parents' rights to custody.

Invasion of a family's privacy and rights of governance begins as soon as the state investigates a report of child abuse, continues when it removes a child from parental custody, and concludes when it acts to sever permanently the ties between parents and children.

The removal of children from their biological home can be done in an instant the moment the social worker or police see danger to the health and safety of the children. It can be done subsequent to a hearing (typically held seventy-two hours after the social service agency files a care-and-protection petition in a juvenile court). Parents whose children have just been, or are about to be, removed have three explicit rights. They have the right to notice of a hearing, to be present at the hearing, to confront and cross-examine witnesses. The same rights are part of termination hearings.

"Termination of parental rights" is a dry legal concept. It represents the final step in governmental intrusion. To terminate parental rights, the state must show that the consequences of allowing the parent-child relationship to continue are more severe than the consequences of terminating that relationship. Courts must apply a "fitness standard." They must be able to establish that a parent is not only unfit, but also unfit for a specific child. And following a 1982 Supreme Court case, *Santosky v. Kramer*, the standard of unfitness had to be proved by "clear and convincing evidence." This is a higher standard, requiring more proof than "preponderance of the evidence," a standard of proof used in less critical matters.

The *Santosky* case reflected a series of studies of the child-welfare system in the seventies. The first of the studies indicated that the rights of parents, particularly non-English-speaking parents, were being routinely ignored. The studies were also highly critical of social service agencies' failure to provide the kind of services to parents that might enable them to retain or regain custody of their children. Readers already know that the studies produced federal dollars for programs that brought homemaker and parent support into private homes.

Readers are also aware of the increase of poverty, drug abuse, and violent crime in the eighties and nineties. The social service agencies were overwhelmed. They lost staff and suffered high turnover. The programs described above were too limited to be effective in this more violent climate. A rash of sensationalized cases in the media depicted the risks to individual children who were left in the care of abusive families. The public clamored for more aggressive child protection. In these cases, the rights of parents and rights of children came into direct conflict.

Our society turns to the courtroom, clumsy and unsatisfying though it may be, to provide the only sanctioned space for resolving conflict. But the pace of courtroom activity in these two decades overwhelmed the juvenile court systems in the same way that the social service agencies had been overwhelmed. Juvenile courts did not have adequate personnel or courtroom space, and they often lacked full-time administrators. Juvenile court judges were, as always, randomly selected and poorly trained. Some juvenile sessions took place in district court settings with judges who regarded the need to preside over a juvenile session as a nuisance. They brought boredom, ignorance, and irritation to their task. The inability of the social service agencies to operate effectively, the apparent indifference of some juvenile court judges, and a client community which seemed to be destroying itself with more drugs and more violence combined to create even more cases of severe child neglect and abuse. Newspapers increasingly published graphic news of the deaths of children at the hands of biological parents, abuse in foster homes, and, again, children languishing in foster care for far too long.

Children in the custody of the Department of Social Services (DSS) are required by federal law to have their cases reviewed in court every six months. Many foster care review cases, however, were indefinitely delayed because untrained district court judges did not want to deal with them. The cases did not move forward to resolution, so the children remained in placement limbo. As observed earlier, they remain in "foster care drift."

The same 1997 Adoption and Safe Families Act (ASFA) that gave social service agencies money to increase the number and speed of adoptions came to the rescue of the courts. The legislation gave money to court administrators to bring order, efficiency, and innovation to the courtrooms. The results in Massachusetts have been very encouraging. There are now thirty-seven juvenile court judges, up from twelve in 1994. Juvenile sessions are no longer held in district courts. All care-and-protection cases are held in juvenile courts with trained judges and uniform rules of procedure. DSS and the judges are supposed to follow the same "risk-factor matrix" guide when deciding what level of abuse leads to the removal of a child, thus producing some consistency among courts. The courts are now responsible, along with the agencies, to end foster care drift and to bring cases to a resolution with "all deliberate speed." However, Massachusetts' juvenile courts find it difficult to comply with the mandate because of the way clients are represented; the lawyers who represent children or parents in the juvenile court maintain private, more lucrative practices outside the court. Their scheduling preferences take precedence over juvenile court needs. A better method of providing lawyers is suggested later in this chapter.

Juvenile court probation departments have developed innovative programs to assist children before they become involved in serious crime. Examples of these programs include the Fatherhood Program, the Firesetters Program, the Teenage Criminal Justice Academy, Clean Slate, the Non-judicial Delinquency Diversion Program, Operation Night Ride, and the Alternative Sentencing Project. Probation departments are also working with school departments to

reduce truancy, assigning full time probation officers to school. With additional federal money from the Court Improvement Project, the juvenile courts
have been able to join with the Department of Mental Health to provide a system of juvenile court clinics to serve the various juvenile court divisions. A
team headed by a psychiatrist staffs the clinics. At the judge's request they con-
duct evaluations on either parent or child depending on the issue and case that
is before the court. Evaluations frequently include recommendations for intervention and treatment, providing a valuable resource to judges.

The emphasis of ASFA lay squarely behind child safety and child well-
being. This placed a special burden on the courts. They have two separate, conflicting tasks. First, mindful of the abuse of parental rights that prevailed
before the era of *Gault* they have the task of pressing social services to keep the
family in tact, so that no child is removed who should have remained home.
Then, they must reverse priorities and scrutinize the evidence presented by the
department, challenging it if need be, in order to determine whether the child
can safely remain in her home, or should be in a foster-care placement. An
activist judiciary is an essential element in a quality child-protection system.

Courts are also obligated to enter an area of child protection controversy
where they are reluctant to go. This is the area that presents itself when a
gravely ill child requires medical treatment that the child's parents are refusing
to give. These cases are difficult and sensitive, in part because many involve
fundamental constitutional rights, such as religious freedom and personal privacy. A 1978 Massachusetts case lays bare these conflicting rights, where
human emotion and the life of a child fight for space in a court of law.

The Massachusetts Supreme Judicial Court was called upon to adjudicate
the case of Chad Green, a very young boy with acute lymphocytic leukemia.
His doctors had prescribed a course of chemotherapy that they thought would

provide a substantial cure or long-term remission of the disease. The parents wished to replace this treatment with a regimen involving the use of laetrile, a substance of highly questionable value. A trial judge found the minor to be in need of care and protection and issued an order requiring the parents to allow the child to undergo chemotherapy; legal custody was vested in the Department of Public Welfare for the limited purpose of assuring that the medical treatment was administered.

The parents appealed. The Supreme Judicial Court began by restating the old principles: there is a private realm of family life which the state cannot enter; parents are the natural guardians of their children, with the primary right to raise their children according to the dictates of their consciences. The Chief Justice wrote as follows,

> It is also well established, however, that the parental rights described above do not clothe parents with life and death authority over their children. This court has stated that the parental right to control a child's nurture is grounded not in any absolute property right which can be enforced to the detriment of the child, but rather is akin to a trust, subject to a correlative duty to care for and protect the child, and terminable by the parents' failure to discharge their obligations.

In spite of the high possibility of remission and a normal childhood with chemotherapy, the parents decided that his chances were better with laetrile. They took him to Mexico for a series of laetrile treatments, where he died. There was some discussion among child-welfare advocates about whether the parents would be held in criminal contempt when they returned to the state. The Judge, observing that they had suffered enough, held them in contempt, but imposed neither a fine nor a jail sentence.

In a second Massachusetts case, the family withheld all medical treatment because they were Christian Scientists who relied exclusively on prayer for a cure. Their son, Robyn Twitchell, suffered from a congenital defect that had caused a bowel obstruction. The Twitchells were informed that without medical intervention Robyn would suffer a certain and painful death. The parents refused; Robyn suffered and died. A jury subsequently convicted them of recklessly and wantonly causing Robyn's death. The presiding judge placed the Twitchells on ten years probation and ordered them to take their three surviving children to periodic health check-ups under the guidelines set by the American Medical Association. She observed that religious convictions do not exempt parents from fulfilling this essential responsibility for their children.

Thus the thin line is drawn between the protection of child health and parental rights. Lawyers who represent parents in court are uncomfortable with the line, fearing that one erosion of the line will lead to others. At the moment, Massachusetts is one of only eight states that tilt firmly against parents' rights in these matters, but the trend is going in the direction Massachusetts has taken. The United States Supreme Court once wrote that parents do not have an absolute right to deny their children medical treatment on religious grounds. "…while the parents may be free to become martyrs themselves, it does not follow that they are free, in identical circumstances, to make martyrs of their children." The secular public supports this line and supports putting the responsibility for defining and enforcing the line in the hands of judges. Judges tread where clergymen once walked.

Family Courts

Do juvenile courts represent "the highest form of justice" (Dean of Harvard Law School, 1940) or "the worst of both worlds" (Justice Abe Fortas, 1967)?

As we have already seen, federal legislation (ASFA) has given juvenile judges a very full plate. They are in charge of reviewing the work of social service agencies, resulting in more frequent and longer court hearings. The poverty- and drug-induced disintegration of the urban American family has led over 400,000 children into court for care and protection proceedings. Twenty years ago, judges saw half that number.

Juvenile judges are required to perform a long list of tasks. The judges are asked to be social workers, bringing information from the disciplines of psychology and sociology to bear on their decisions about child maltreatment and removal. They are mandated to oversee the work of the agency itself, to review the social worker's plan for reunification or for permanent placement outside the home, and to monitor the services the agency uses, from bonding studies to parenting clinics. In the last two decades of the twentieth century, the judge's' role expanded beyond the expansion it experienced in the thirties and forties.

What follows is an argument that this expanded role be acknowledged and expanded further. This will require better trained and better paid judges, and vastly more court personnel. It is an argument for family courts. Family courts are currently found statewide in eight states and in local districts in four others.

What is a family court?

The basic element of any court system is jurisdiction. Current court organization, with some exceptions, typically places three child-centered events under a juvenile court's jurisdiction: abuse and neglect petitions, juvenile status offenders (non-criminal delinquents), and delinquents who commit non-violent crimes such as shoplifting. Some juveniles who commit violent crimes will also be tried in juvenile court. But if the prosecuting district attorney believes the crime to be sufficiently serious he will demand a transfer to an adult court. The remainder of the court activity that involves children is usually under the jurisdiction of a probate court.

Probate courts began as courts that handled wills and estates. The twentieth century has added divorce, child custody, adoptions, international child custody disputes, paternity testing, collection of money owed by delinquent fathers to their divorced wives, and trials for termination of parental rights.

Court reorganization would take all matters affecting families and children and place them in a unified family court, leaving only common-law issues like the probing of wills and estates to probate courts. The National Council of Juvenile and Family Judges, a prime mover for family courts, offers any or all of the following items for the jurisdiction of a family court: abuse and neglect allegations, adoption, juvenile delinquency, juvenile status offenses, child custody and visitation, review of children in placement, termination of parental rights trials, dissolution of marriage, alimony, child support, paternity questions, domestic violence, spousal abuse, elder abuse, and management of minors' funds.

Experience shows that a successful family court has to be managed by committed, specialized judges. Most importantly, these judges have to be dedicated to improving the lives of the children who come before them. Of course, there is the danger that history will repeat itself, and that unbridled power over children and their families will bring back the abuses of the recent past. However, the court has assumed such importance in the lives of children in child-protective services that it only makes sense to acknowledge the extended authority and give it the legal and technical assistance required. Due process protection will come from conscientious lawyers and from a more informed citizenry.

There are several ways of organizing these courts. The most common method is to put one judge in charge of a specific set of families; the judge then hears all matters in which the family is involved. Some jurisdictions add a magistrate or lesser hearing officer to this picture. Others add a whole treatment team. The psychological evaluations and other services then become a more integrated part of the permanency plan. The goal is to keep one case-managing judge and one family together for every court proceeding in which the family is involved (except for violent crime). Modifications can be put in place in the interest of fairness: for example, Oregon juvenile judges excuse themselves from a termination trial if they have heard the initial evidence alleging abuse and neglect.

The advantages of a family court are many. Family court judges control their own calendars, so they are in charge of scheduling the hearings and trials in their courtroom. This reduces the current plague of trials broken into pieces over days or weeks. They can more easily coordinate the services they order, such as mental-health evaluation or supervised visitation. Family court judges cast their information net wide. They have more data with which to shape an individualized disposition for a case. This is especially important when presented with delinquents who are first-time non-violent offenders.

The greatest gift a unified family court gives the families is invisible. Through some form of alchemy it unleashes the imagination of the presiding judges; they become creative project designers, making use of every federal dollar available and figuring out how to obtain grant money. Some of their projects are expensive. There is, for example, the expanded use of social service agencies. In Delaware, the child-protection agency always has representatives in the court, and their offices are in the court building. In Jefferson City, Kentucky, each judge has a social worker on staff who is present in the courtroom and assists in making decisions, while simultaneously getting needed services to the families. The Jefferson City school system has two liaison persons to inform the court about school-related issues. Family court judges make excellent use of CASAs.[12] Several judges have brought truancy courts right into the middle school buildings, holding them in the early morning hours once a week. Judges have experimented with holding court at night or on the weekend, trying to accommodate the needs of parents who work.

A truly inspiring program is in its early stages in Durham, North Carolina. Judge Kenneth C. Titus has pooled public and private grant money to create a management team. He was able to hire four new staff people, one of whom develops and monitors the outside resources needed by the court, another of whom works primarily on finding new grants. Judge Titus believes that he is in charge of every aspect of the life of the families who appear before him. In that mode, he might subpoena the Superintendent of Schools into the courtroom and ask him if he was aware that one of his teachers had the habit of sending a ten-year-old boy home every morning because he caused trouble in class. Judge Titus envisions a full-service court. He wants a drug treatment center attached to the court that will include drug counseling. He wants the court to offer life-skill training, job assistance, connection to housing programs, day care, parenting classes, and supervised visitation.

His enthusiasm is infectious, causing listeners to entertain thoughts of nationwide imitation. Of course, it is the charisma of the Judge Titus and his commitment to the well-being of children that creates the atmosphere of success.

Recalling the disastrous consequences when the benign paternalism of Judge Ben Lindsay (Denver Court, 1899) became the abandonment of due process in the hands of later judges, this author feels cautious about placing a

---

[12] CASA stands for Court Appointed Special Advocate. CASA was founded in 1977 in the King County Superior Court in Washington to meet the need for more effective advocacy for children. It is a nationwide organization, relying primarily on volunteers. CASAs are an arm of the court, and report directly to a judge.

lot of power into the hands of one juvenile court judge. However, 2000 is noticeably different from 1900. Both government and private organizations perform minimal watchdog services, calling attention to judicial abuses. Most courts provide attorneys for indigent parents and interpreters for non-English-speaking parents. These safeguards should protect the weakest parents from the kinds of abuse they once suffered. What is very clear is that our times demand a top-down organization, a case management that only a family court can provide, and a close supervision of the social service agencies that only a family court can provide. The court alone has the authority to enforce an order for services, to challenge the permanent plan written by a social worker, or to ensure essential contact between court, school, and health care provider.

Critics say that it is not right to ask an ordinary judge to turn himself into a child development expert. But "ordinary judges" are asked to preside over complex medical malpractice trials, product liability trials, and anti-trust trials in which extremely technical matters are at issue. Certainly, the issues in a child abuse trial would not be more difficult, particularly for specially-trained judges.

There is also the often-voiced fear of judge burnout. One child abuse case after another, it is said, will begin to erode a judge's ability to be impartial. But family law is not "one child abuse case after another." It involves a range of issues, and an occasional warm moment (adoptions). Judges who preside over nothing but business contract disputes also have a potential burnout problem. Remember that no one is forced to be a judge, or a judge in a family court.

Finally, opponents say that you do not have to turn over the whole apple cart to get court improvements. We have already seen what innovations Massachusetts has been able to achieve using federal funds and legislature grants. But there is a continuing need for better organization of the court, a more unified approach to clients, and tighter control over the unruly and unreviewable Department of Social Services. Over a ten-year period the Governor's Commission on the Unmet Legal Needs of Children, The Boston Bar Association, the Massachusetts Supreme Judicial Court Report on Juvenile Justice, and the federal and state Departments of Health and Human Services have concurred that Massachusetts should have a family court. However, the judges who sit in the Massachusetts Probate and Juvenile Courts uniformly reject a family court for the state or the city of Boston, including one judge who sat on a national panel that issued a report calling for unified family courts! There is a firm, widespread belief that the Massachusetts judiciary is fixed in its old, venerated ways (after all, the Massachusetts Supreme Judicial Court is older than the United States Supreme Court) and that the Massachusetts state legislature would never commit the amount of funding the project would need.

This is unfortunate. Most studies of failed social service agencies agree that improved services for children in need of protection can only come through judicial leadership. The state judiciary and the state legislatures should strike boldly. The twenty-first century should be the century in which juvenile justice comes into its own. A visionary family court judge with a supportive staff could put meaning into the phrase "juvenile justice."

CHAPTER TEN

The Massachusetts Department of Social Services

1970–2000

The Massachusetts Department of Social Services

1970–2000

Introduction

The nation stands fully behind a policy of child protection. Americans will fund any program that promises to end the "national nightmare" of child abuse and neglect. Their horror at the details of an especially brutal story of abuse turns to anger at the child-protective services. The public does do not know how a protective agency works, but one thing they do know: its record is one egregious failure after another. Regrettably, the child-protective agency itself is often confused about its mandate, and reacts to highly publicized failures with defensive maneuvers that are designed not to serve families but to ward off further criticism.

It is clear that child-protective services are overwhelmed by the scope and complexity of their task. Substance abuse among parents, rates of family breakup, deepening pockets of poverty, and cuts in government services have intensified family problems and reduced options for helping. In 1995, nearly three million children were reported to be possible victims of child abuse or neglect—triple the number of reports made just twenty years earlier. By 1999, half a million children were in foster care nationwide, a 9% growth over the preceding nine-year period. Child-protection Services (henceforth designated as CPS) unable to adjust to the growing demand have been awarded "the dubi-ous distinction of being among the most maligned public agencies."[13]

In 1991, the National Commission on Children charged, "If the nation had deliberately designed a system that would frustrate the professionals who staff it, anger the public who finance it, and abandon the children who depend on it, it could not have done a better job than the present child-welfare system."

Expected to straddle two core values of American society—the protection of children and respect for the privacy of the family—CPS are accused of both unwarranted interference with parental prerogatives, and irresponsible inac-tion when child safety is at issue. But, because children's lives are at stake, CPS cannot stop working while the public debates its mission. "The plane must be fixed while it flies through the air." (Packard Foundation)

What follows is a close look at one child-protection agency, the Massachusetts Department of Social Services (DSS or "the department"). It will focus on Boston, the most populous city in the state.

---

[13] This quote and a great deal of other information in this introductory section can be found in *The Future of Children, Protecting Children from Abuse and Neglect*, The David and Lucy Packard Foundation.

Massachusetts Department of Social Services

The predecessor of DSS, the Department of Public Welfare (DPW), came into being in 1919. It was the state's first child-protection agency. No political event ruffled its sleepy existence for the next forty years. It existed largely to provide financial assistance to those thought worthy of a welfare check; it was staffed largely by kindly bookkeepers and administered in the local offices of the cities and towns. Those who wished to communicate with the DPW went to a local office where the staff was housed.

Dr. C. Henry Kempe's report on child abuse (see Chapter Eight), published in 1962, stirred this quiet world. Although physicians were the first mandated reporters, child-welfare professionals began to suspect that many cases of child abuse and neglect were not being reported.

Massachusetts Governor Frank Sargent established the Committee on Child Abuse in 1970 to address that problem. A survey of physicians and hospitals revealed that physicians were hesitant to report abuse or neglect. The committee therefore proposed new and more expansive mandatory reporting language. One objective of the proposal was to identify the families of children at risk so that they could receive services that would reduce harm to children. The committee was also motivated by recent federal legislation that made federal funds conditional on the adoption by states of more effective measures to prevent child abuse and neglect. In 1973, Massachusetts adopted the present 51A system of mandated reporting which, among other things, vastly expanded the list of mandated reporters.[14]

---

[14] "51A" is shorthand for the Massachusetts reporting statute on child abuse. Immediately after receiving a "51A" phone call or report, DSS is mandated to investigate.

The number of reports grew ten fold in the seventies. The increase in reported cases severely taxed the capacities of the DPW, which became responsible for child welfare as well as for dispensing welfare payments. In 1974, the federal government ruled that the two functions, protecting child welfare and dispensing welfare checks, had to be separately administered. Thus, the Massachusetts practice of combining clerks and a few "social workers" into one public-assistance agency was no longer acceptable.

Massachusetts gave an exam to all current DPW workers, and, according to their scores, permitted them to select their future position—either in Social Services in the newly created Division of Child Guardianship (DCG) or in Assistance Payments. Employees were also awarded significant points for longevity in employment. Thus bookkeepers were transformed into "social workers" who had neither training, experience, nor special interest in child-protection work. But the seventies ushered in the era of more serious child abuse and neglect. As previously indicated, the number of difficult cases accelerated. This patched-together unit was not prepared to meet the challenge. Highly publicized deaths of children under the care of the DCG signaled the severity of the problem. One of these cases concerned a woman who had been in foster care all of her life, *Denise Gallison.*

Denise, one of five siblings born to parents with histories of mental retardation and prison terms for petty crimes, had been through eleven foster care homes and institutional placements by the time she was discharged from the custody of DCG in 1978, at age eighteen.

Her social worker's discharge notes describe a very immature girl, mildly retarded, unable to hold a job for longer than one day. At the time of discharge she was living with a thirty-two-year-old boyfriend, John Deats[15], who was

---

[15] With the exception of Denise Gallison, all other names in this case are fictitious.

married and had two children. Deats was also diagnosed as either mildly retarded or just "very slow."

Three weeks after discharge she applied to DPW for public assistance, announcing that she was pregnant. She added that her boyfriend was only in the apartment some of the time (and that when he was there he liked to beat her up "a little bit"). Catholic Charities, on contract with DPW, assumed responsibility for her and her expected baby.

From the date of the birth of her son, Billy, on November 4, 1974, through the birth of her daughter, Jennifer, on September 23, 1975, until she was led away to jail in May, 1978, Denise and her family had been the subject of the following: a Visiting Nurse Association report that the children were without diapers and wrapped in rags, and two separate court investigation reports concluding that the "...son, Billy, was mistreated physically and emotionally." Several different social workers and supervisors in two separate agencies (Catholic Charities and Division of Child Guardianship) reported variously that the children were in terrible condition or that Denise was learning how to take care of her children and they were doing well.

There were seven separate court review hearings, designed to give the judge hearing the case an opportunity to monitor the welfare of children over whom the DCG had custody. There were verbal and written reports by Billy's foster mother, talking about how severely bruised he was every time he returned to her after a weekend with his mother and father.

On March 20, 1978, an anonymous report of a crying child was phoned into the local DCG office. The social worker assigned to the case, Margaret Fields, went to the home on March 20 and on March 21. No one was home. Fields did not ask the neighbors about the whereabouts of the family. She did not try to ascertain whether anyone had seen the children. She left a note for

Denise asking her to call. On March 22 Denise called to say she had been in a neighboring town because of a death in one of her former foster families and that she would be returning. Fields noted that Denise sounded "good, calm."

On April 7, 1978, Denise called the worker, who entered this note in her Quarterly Assessment Report, dated April 28, 1978: "During the conversation of 4-7-78, D. informed worker that family was moving on 4-8-78 to her "mother's" home in New Bedford (MA). Mother also informed Assistant Director that she was expecting another child in August." Fields further noted in the Quarterly Assessment Report form of 4-28: "Billy has been well since his return home. D. decided his earlier problems were caused by allergy to dog fur. Jennifer is reported to be twenty-nine pounds. D. describes her as getting tall and slender, like her father. Jennifer (almost three) is toilet trained during the day, but still wears Pampers at night. Mother reports that Jennifer eats and sleeps well and has stayed healthy."

At the time of this telephone conversation, Jennifer had been dead for two and one half months.

Jennifer had been killed, accidentally, during a drunken fight between Denise and Deats. They had kept the dead body in the house for six weeks. Shortly before Easter, they had chopped her limbs from her body and put the contents in a box in a park.

On April 28, the Assistant Director wrote to Denise informing her that since she was moving to New Bedford, her case would be transferred there. On May 12, an anonymous caller complained to both the police and the DCG of child abuse at the family's apartment. Fields was confused, thinking the family had moved to New Bedford. The police met her at the family's apartment. Fields asked to see the children. Denise refused entry. She said the children were not there. Denise called her husband home from work. When Deats let the police and Fields into the apartment, they found the Billy sitting on a chair, seriously injured. He was covered with bruises and had no lower lip. Denise later explained that he kept asking her, "Where's Jenny? Where's Jenny?" She couldn't stand listening to him so she beat him. Jennifer could not be found. Deats said she was in Texas with his parents. Billy was taken to the police station to be photographed, then to the hospital.

The investigative committee that revealed the details of this case concluded, "It is reported that this child lived in an apartment with the body of his dead sister for six weeks; his parents made him stand in a corner with dirty underwear over his head; they burned him with cigarettes; he was so badly beaten, his lower lip was obliterated. No one can assess the damage to his psyche. We can only say that after all the damage has been squeezed from this story, he will still be left with these memories of terror."

The parents of these children are in jail and the principle social worker was fired. Billy's foster mother, Marie Molson, adopted him.

In response to the crises created by this case and others, the governor and legislature created a separate child-protection agency, which would focus entirely on child-welfare issues, particularly child-protective services. Because the use of untrained clerks had had such devastating results, *the legislation included a prohibition against "grandfathering" unqualified staff into the new agency.* (The emphasis is the author's.)

While the legislature created the new agency in three months, two years passed before it opened its doors to the public. Placed within the Executive Office of Human Services, the Department of Social Services was charged with fifteen separate tasks organized around counseling, protective services, development of adoption, day care, foster care, residential centers, homemaker services, referral services, and training for parents. The legislation required the commissioner to establish reasonable caseloads (between fifteen and eighteen per worker) and a management and information system. The department was further directed to help develop client resources, work toward professionaliz- ing its social workers, and establish interagency relationships between DSS, DPW, the Department of Mental Health, and the Department of Youth Services (juvenile delinquency).

Presented now is a restatement of the questions first asked in chapter one. The first child-protection agency's director posed them in 1919. He said the public could measure its success by asking five questions: Has it protected and made happier the unfortunate and neglected children of the Commonwealth? Have individuals, officials, and other societies turned to it with a better under- standing of its purposes and its power to render service? Has its staff become more sensitive to the abuses of children, and at the same time become more intelligent in the use of all the social, medical, and legal remedies that our com- munities provide? Has it contributed to a better understanding of the condi- tions that continue to wreck or maim children's lives? Has it learned to dovetail its work with that of other agencies so as to reduce duplication and increase effectiveness?

The 1919 agency failed in its mission. The answer to all the questions was "No." Over time it lost its individuality and vanished into the vast maw of the Department of Public Welfare, to become nothing more than a distributor of checks, inadvertently destroying rather than protecting child welfare. What would be the fate of its reincarnation as The Department of Social Services?

On July 1, 1980, DSS began providing services. At first the new department seemed to be working well, but soon it was assaulted by one crisis after another. Cases sensationalized by the media focused public scrutiny on the department, which then reacted defensively. The department's problems were further complicated by litigation. First, Greater Boston Legal Services filed a federal class-action suit, the result of which was an unfunded court mandate that DSS reduce its worker caseload. Next, the Massachusetts Committee for Children and Youth, (MCCY) brought a suit on behalf of the abused and neglected children of the Commonwealth. The department fought the suit for four years, but judges would not dismiss it because stories of horrible child abuse kept surfacing in the city's newspapers. Finally, the parties entered into a consent decree on August 1, 1984. In return for the suspension of the litigation, the department promised (among other things):

- To control the caseload number for on-line case workers (not yet achieved).
- To develop a set of training manuals (which it did in 1997, thirteen years later).
- To give foster parents training (only recently achieved).
- To make DSS responsible for the health needs of all the children in their custody (achieved).

The Boston media, principally the major newspaper, *The Boston Globe*, continued throughout the eighties to publicize the deaths of children in foster care or at the hands of their parents after DSS had returned them home from their foster-care placements. DSS Commissioners changed, but nothing helped.

To try to tame the beast of the foster care crisis (see Chapter Nine) Governor Michael Dukakis appointed a special commission to investigate the problems and make recommendations. The commission called for an increase in payments to foster parents, mandatory training for foster parents, and the recruitment of hundreds of additional foster parents. The Report was well received by those who read it, but ignored.

The slashing of welfare budgets during eight years of the Reagan presidency resulted in a series of budget crises for the states. The department's budget was cut and the number of workers reduced. At the same time, incomes in the lower third of American households fell and the number of abuse cases grew. From 1983 to 1991, the number of 51A reports filed increased from approximately 35,000 to 90,000. The department was handling twice the number of active cases it had eight years earlier with a staff constantly reduced by burnout and low pay (they received no pay raise in the eighties). In 1988, workers struck over the size of their caseloads. Management negotiated a settlement whereby no social worker's caseload would exceed twenty-two (Note that the MCCY's suit in 1984 had been settled at "no more than eighteen cases per worker"). The ink on the agreement was not yet dry when further budget cuts *reduced* staff size.

The department had no choice but to contract casework out to private providers, such as Catholic Charities, Boston Children's Service, and Alianza Hispaña.

Once casework went outside of the department, it lost the last semblance of consistency in delivery of services or quality control.

The nineties opened very much like the eighties. From 1990 to 1992, the department's caseload increased by 2%, while its budget shrank by 4%. DSS appeared to be completely dysfunctional. One could not ascertain who was in charge, where the lines of authority were. There still was no training for newly hired social workers, and the training for foster parents was moving slowly. Within the first six months of 1990, fifty-two children in DSS custody died. Instances of terrible misjudgment splashed across the pages of the *Globe*. Reporters learned that two sisters were repeatedly raped in a home from which DSS had once removed the children. They had returned them to the home and closed the case. Two weeks later, readers of the *Globe* were treated to the story of "Mikey" Sanborn. Mikey was a child who had been with one foster family for all of his eight years, but who was arbitrarily whisked away—with no warning—at the close of a therapy session. He was whisked away not because he was in danger, but because he was the victim of bureaucratic tug of war within the department.[16]

The *Globe* revelations continued unabated. September 1, 1991: "Foster Care System Seen in Disarray; Commissioner Replaced." This was the third replacement since 1980; this one lasted less than a year. Two weeks later: "Abused Child Faces More Abuse in System." The article chronicled the maddening delay between the discovery of severe physical abuse and the final freeing of a child for adoption. Eric was one year old and had sustained a broken leg and dislocated shoulder at the hands of his mother. But, after three years, two foster homes, and nineteen hearings, he had still not been freed for adoption. By December of 1991 a consensus of legislators, child advocates, and the public was forming to "do something." Also by December 1991, severe budget slashes had cut the heart out of every program that served the poor, such as AFDC, housing benefits, the Department of Social Services. After clamor by the public and the media, the governor and legislature agreed to put $4 million into an emergency fund for DSS. And because commissioning studies is easier than actually finding solutions, Governor William Weld commissioned another study.

As the reader is aware, the previous governor, Michael Dukakis, had already commissioned a study. All the right people—lawyers, judges, social workers—worked

---

[16] The *Globe*, like all newspapers, prints sensational headlines before it knows all the facts, and is indifferent to nuances. Nonetheless, it remains a roughly reliable reporter of DSS events.

hard to evaluate the problems and propose solutions. As the reader is also aware, it sat unheralded and unread on the desks of many important people.

At the time this second study was commissioned in 1992, the public and the press were far more exercised about diagnosing DSS' problems and proposing solutions. Titled "Special Commission on Foster Care," the report was much more than that. The commission endeavored to examine the system from every participant's point of view. It included foster parents, former foster children, legislators, child-welfare professionals, representatives of DSS, a representative of the Executive Office of Health and Human Services (the executive arm under which DSS operates), a representative of the state auditor, representatives of private-provider agencies, and child-welfare advocates. A highly-respected Boston attorney, Gael Mahoney, chaired it.[17]

As to the quality of services DSS delivered to children, the Mahoney Report found that children in DSS custody were exposed to repeated abuse and neglect, and that DSS records were disorganized and chaotic, and did not reflect adequate diagnosis or systematic planning for children. Further, it found that children were placed at risk because vital clinical information about critical matters, such as addictive parental behavior or spousal abuse, was not utilized and translated into case practice. The commission concluded that as a result of those multiple failures by DSS, the children in the DSS system suffered increasing developmental failures and behavioral disturbances.

The commission report described DSS as an agency in the midst of an organizational breakdown. "In the face of worsening crises in its caseload, loss of public confidence, and a groundswell of demands for fundamental and comprehensive reform, the department stood virtually paralyzed." Although its leadership was weak and ineffective, imminent collapse was averted by the

---

[17] Information recorded here can be found in "Special Commission on Foster Care," Volumes I-III.

dedication of its workers and staff. "Despite being assailed by the press, deprived of needed resources, unsupported by management, and overloaded with critical cases, the DSS workers continue to deal daily with the most difficult and soul-searing problems we face as a society."

The commission noted that for twelve years the department had failed to carry out its mandate. It then offered over twenty recommendations that it felt were necessary to create an agency that could protect children. Among them were recommendations to streamline social workers' tasks with a new computerized information system, to reduce their workload and permit flexibility for complex cases, and to encourage and provide the means for professional development. Further, the commission suggested that DSS work with the legislature to attract social workers with master's degrees by offering higher pay.

In addition, the commission urged the creation of a multi-disciplinary team to assess the risk to a child at the time the case opened. This would reduce the problems that resulted from faulty judgment at the very beginning. They said DSS' sham Fair Hearing review procedure had to be replaced with an honest one, because such a review was one of the very few ways a client could challenge a decision. The list continued: DSS needed a better ethnic mix in its staff, a more thorough review of its system of awarding contracts, and readily-available mental-health services. It needed to treat foster parents as true partners of the department and have better interagency cooperation and information-sharing. Finally, the department had to undertake an immediate "revenue maximization effort." *The commission estimated that an additional $40 to $70 million in federal reimbursements would be available if properly claimed.* In other words, DSS had to be reinvented, and money for this reinvention was available.

DSS did not reinvent itself. At first, one could see no changes at all. In 1994, a frightening case of child abuse took place under the negligent eyes of a DSS-contracted agency. A family of six children with a drug-addicted mother had been transferred from DSS to Alianza Hispaña. This agency had no particular expertise in child abuse and no trained social workers. The mother and her boyfriend punished one of her sons, four-year-old Ernesto, by holding his hands under scalding water until all the skin came off. To be certain that no one found could learn of this act, they locked him in a room for two days, where he lay, soaked in his own blood, urine, and excrement. Relief came when a family member who could no longer tolerate knowing about this called the police. DSS terminated their contract with Alianza, and the mother and boyfriend went to prison. But there were six children in that family, one with hands he would never be able to use fully again. Their profound distress would not be cured by the jail sentence nor by the only response available to DSS, terminating its contract with Alianza.

Lest the reader suspect that the *Boston Globe* was resorting to sensationalism to generate newspaper headlines, I will relate a few of my own experiences and those of two of my colleagues at the Boston Juvenile Court. Recall the procedure in Massachusetts: attorneys are appointed by a juvenile court judge to represent either parents or children who have been named on a DSS petition filed in court alleging abuse or neglect. The judge appoints an attorney from a list maintained by a public agency called Committee for Public Counsel Services (CPCS). CPCS was formerly a Public Defenders Agency and had a staff of lawyers who dealt exclusively with adult criminal matters. The current CPCS has expanded to include the training and certifying of private attorneys who represent indigent parties named on care-and-protection petitions, juvenile delinquents, and indigent mentally-ill clients in need of advocacy. The private attorneys who receive their appointments through the juvenile court earn $39.00 an hour, a fee that is ultimately paid by the state government.

If the CPCS attorney is representing one of the parents, her position is adversarial to the DSS attorney. Representing a child is different; the lawyer for the child may choose to work with, or against, the DSS attorney, depending on her perception of whether DSS' position is in the child's best interest.

I am not relating the details of these cases for the purpose of generating another set of lurid stories. Nor do I wish to impugn the efforts of the many dedicated and under-supported people who struggle and give their utmost to help their clients in a dysfunctional system. Rather, I hope to illustrate the futility of the present approach by giving the reader the details of stories that reveal where DSS fails in its protective mission.

As we read these devastating stories we need to keep our minds focused on the recurring themes which are laced through them. The first problems lie in the selection and efficient use of the on-line social worker and the supervisory staff. This includes too much crucial judgment left in the hands of young, inexperienced workers, poor quality review of their decisions, lack of technical support, and policy-mandated misuse of workers' time. Another problem stems from institutional biases, including a bias against fathers and against attorneys who represent parents. The department does not really approve of parents having legal representation. It extends this disapproval to the attorneys who represent the parents. This leads the agency to put up roadblocks to attorneys seeking information, even relatively unimportant information.

The most persistent theme of the following case histories is the autocratic power exercised by the department over clients and their attorneys. Their decisions have enormous impact on the families who are involved with them, much of what they do is behind closed doors, and their decisions are virtually unreviewable.

All the names of the parties in these cases have been changed.

Case 1: The Broder Children

| Children: | Mary Broder | Date of Birth: 9-2-82 |
| | Lois Broder | Date of Birth: 5-14-84 |

| Mother: | Rose Iminez |
| Father: | Joe Broder |

| Race: | Hispanic-Black |

I represented the children in this case. The case opened in 1986. I was appointed to represent the children in 1989, after their first appointed attorney moved out of state.

On October 1, 1986, the paternal grandmother and a neighbor called the DSS hotline with a report of child abuse. An emergency DSS worker went to the apartment where the girls lived, accompanied by police from the local precinct.

The DSS worker was told that when the two little girls were visiting the grandmother, a neighbor's eighteen-year-old daughter had taken two-year-old Lois to the bathroom. When she pulled down her underpants, the child screamed in pain because her underpants were stuck to her buttocks. There were raw areas on the sides of her buttocks that looked like bites and burns. The children told the grandmother and the neighbor that Phil Kapo, their mother's current boyfriend, bit Lois.

A DSS social worker met with the mother, Ms. Iminez, and the two children. She observed that Lois had what looked like severe burns on her buttocks and deep bite marks on her left cheek. Both children said Phil Kapo bit and hit her, but Ms. Iminez explained that Lois had "accidentally" fallen against a radiator.

The worker, Francine Cullen, then took mother and children to a hospital. During the hospital visit, further conversation with Ms. Iminez disclosed that she was quite aware of Kapo's frequent biting of Lois. When the hospital staff noted that there were other bite marks on her abdomen and chest, Ms. Iminez broke into convulsive crying, shouting out, "Why don't you bite me—don't bite her!"

The interview with Lois continued. When she was asked if Kapo had touched her "down there," pointing to the vaginal area, she said yes. She was brought to Fransiscan Home for Children for a sexual-abuse evaluation, which was substantiated.

Phil Kapo was immediately arrested and held on bail. Ms. Iminez, six months pregnant with his child, tried to raise money to get him out.

At a hearing at the Boston Juvenile Court on October 6, 1986, with all attorneys present, a petition was filed against mother alleging abuse and neglect, and temporary custody given to DSS. The girls were placed very briefly with Mrs. Hopper, an approved foster parent. Ms. Iminez asked that they be placed with family, so they were moved to the home of a family member. That placement lasted for only two months, as the girls were "badly behaved and too much to handle." In July 1987 they were returned to the home of Mr. and Mrs. Hopper, where they remained for two years.

After the District Attorney obtained testimony from the girls, Kapo was sentenced to six years in jail.

Ms. Iminiez' drug habit grew more severe. Between 1987 and 1994, she bore three more children (for a total of six children with four fathers). From time to time she would ask to see the girls, not appear for scheduled visits, and then disappear for whole blocks of time to an unknown address. This period of her life came to an end in 1994 when she was arrested for selling drugs to an undercover officer while pushing her sleeping children in a carriage. She went to jail, and the three remaining children went into family foster care.

Permanent custody of Mary and Lois was granted to the department on June 25, 1987.

Four months later, November 1987, the supervisor of this case learned from another area office that members of the Hopper household had past criminal records, including assault, battery, and rape. The children, nonetheless, remained with the Hoppers.

A new social worker, Alice Grasso, took over the case in 1988. After each monthly visit she wrote in her notes that the girls were "doing well."

In September 1989, Ms. Hopper withdrew from foster care and Mary and Lois went to a new foster home. Within the first month they began to describe to Ms Worther, their new foster mother, how they had been sexually abused by Ms. Hopper's son Sam during the two years they lived the Hopper home.

When the DSS investigator interviewed the girls, Lois reported that sometimes Mrs. Hopper whipped her with a shoe and a belt. She said, "Sam messed with me and Mary." Lois indicated with dolls and drawings where Sam put his penis in both her and Mary (vaginally and rectally), how Mary bled and cried, and that when Sam put his penis in her mouth it made her want to throw up. The investigator asked, "Did the foster mother know that Sam touched your private parts?" Mary answered that she told her, and that she ordered Sam out of the house. But she continued to use him as a "babysitter." The investigator asked, "How many times did these things happen?" One girl answered, "A hundred times." The other answered, "A thousand times."

At this point in their lives, the two girls, ages five and seven, were familiar with vaginal, rectal, and oral intercourse, knew exactly what ejaculate looked like ("juice"), and knew that there was nothing and no one who could help them end this terrifying experience. How could the worker visit every month and not know that something was wrong? These girls were not hiding this information; they told their next foster mother within a month of moving there. What was Alice Grasso thinking when she took Mary to a doctor because she was bleeding? Furthermore, where was the department's sense of responsibility? After learning of the criminal records of members of the household, the department should have removed the girls, even though it would have meant yet another placement for them. At the very least, these revelations should have elicited great vigilance on the part of DSS. Instead, there seemed to be an almost willful blindness about the girls' lives in that house.

Sam Hopper received a sentence of nine to fifteen years for four counts of rape of a child with force. But his memory lingers on. Lois continued for years to dream that he was getting out of jail and would kill her.

The social worker was not only retained by the department, but she earned a master's degree and received a promotion. She remained the chief social worker on this case until 1997.

The nightmare did not stop. Almost as soon as the girls were placed with the new foster mother, Ms. Worther, Mary fell apart. She exhibited self-destructive behavior, such as attempting to jump out of a window, swallowing metal objects, and cutting herself with sharp objects. She also did a great deal of sexual acting-out (masturbating, taking off her clothes, humping against other people and objects). After one month in the placement, Ms. Worther asked that the girls be removed; Mary was admitted to McLean's Hospital for evaluation of her "suicidal ideation" and other aggressive behaviors (one of the most troubling of which was that she had begun to be very mean to her sister, Lois). She was discharged after thirty days with a diagnosis of attention-deficit hyperactivity disorder, major depression, and post-traumatic stress disorder. When she was discharged the department followed McLean's recommendations, placing her in a well-reputed, structured, therapeutic home for troubled children. She was admitted to this facility in August 1990 and remained until discharged to a specialized foster family in 1997.

Lois, now separated from her sister for the first time, was placed in her fifth foster home, a home where only Spanish was spoken. Lois is English speaking. She remained in this home from July 1990 till the time of the much-postponed trial for termination of parental rights in March 1993. Alice Grasso continued to be her worker.

That trial began in a desultory fashion, since Ms. Iminez did not contest the Complaint for Termination of Parental Rights. The father, as was his right, did contest it. However, he had seen the girls only twice since 1986 and was in prison for burglary and assault with a deadly weapon, so the lawyer representing him could not mount a vigorous argument. DSS recommended two placements to the judge on the first day of trial. The first was that Mary remain at her institution until ready for discharge to a specialized foster home (approximately one more year) and that Lois remain with her current foster mother, Juanita Hernandez, to whom, DSS said, she had bonded.

On the second day of trial I received a very distressed phone call from Chris Maguire, a therapist at Lois' school. Ms. Maguire explained that she had worked with Lois since October 1992 and had always had reservations about the foster mother's care. Ms. Maguire added that she, and others, had a great deal of difficulty communicating their concerns to DSS. The agency did not return phone calls and, when finally contacted, trivialized their concerns.

Chris told a colleague that she wanted to find a lawyer to sue DSS; the colleague said that was not necessary, as Lois already had one. Ms. Maguire obtained my name and phoned me. She told me that she and others at the school believed that Lois was left alone a great deal. For example, a colleague who was also the leader of Lois' Girl Scout troop reported that when she drove Lois back to the apartment after meetings, she found that no one was home. Or, alternatively, Lois said she was told to stay downstairs in an apartment with a male babysitter, whom Lois did not trust. The reason for the urgency of the phone call at this time was that Lois had told Chris Maguire that on the night before, while she was sleeping in bed with the foster mother, a strange man came into the room and had a sexual encounter with the foster mother on the floor of the bedroom.

Chris Maguire filed a 51A against the department, which was substantiated. Other school personnel reported that Ms. Hernandez had separated from her husband and was "seeing men," had a new car, and spent a lot of time driving it around. I wanted to obtain a more accurate reading on whether or not Lois had "bonded" with the foster mother, as DSS was claiming, so I asked Ms. Maguire her impression. She replied, "The sad thing is, Lois has never bonded with anyone."

These issues came to light during the trial. One of Lois' teachers, Carol Moffit, was given permission to address the court. She was very angry. Carol Moffit told tales Lois lacking a warm coat in winter and having insufficient food in her lunch box. She was one of the school staff who had repeatedly tried to get the attention of the department. It was she who related the story of returning late from a field trip only to discover an empty, dark apartment. On that occasion, Ms. Moffit took Lois home to spend the night with her. After her testimony it was clear that Lois could not remain with Ms. Hernandez, and when Ms. Moffit offered to take her into her own home until a good placement could be found, the judge gratefully acquiesced (May, 1993). I mused that this might be the child's first lucky break.

But the department looked upon the placement with a jaundiced eye; there is nothing DSS values more highly than having total control over its placements.

DSS contracted Lois' permanent placement needs to another agency, the Cambridge Family and Children's Services (CFCS). It was they who would perform the necessary assessment and find the appropriate placement. That did not mean, however, that DSS surrendered total control. Bitter experience had taught DSS that a contracted agency must submit regular reports on their progress toward the agreed-upon goal. The result of this arrangement, so efficient on paper, was that each agency did no work on the case, but merely waited for the other to act.

Months elapsed. Lois remained in her "temporary" placement with Ms. Moffit (who, incidentally, had a fulltime job and a family of her own). New DSS personnel, who replaced the old social worker and supervisor, knew nothing about the case; CFCS greeted every one of my phone calls with hostility. It was never clear whether they knew what they were supposed to do, how to do it, or who was in charge. Finally, at the end of February 1994, Ms. Moffit received a surprise phone call telling her that all the necessary paper work and preliminary search work had been done, and a family had been found for Lois.

During the nine months that Ms. Moffit had Lois in her home, both DSS and CFCS turned Ms. Moffit into their enemy. It was not clear why; perhaps they needed a person to blame for their continuing incompetence. Ms. Moffit needed help with this child, who was clingy, angry, and violent towards other children in the household. Instead of help, the department heaped criticism upon Ms. Moffit, implying that her mothering was the source of Lois' disruptive behavior.

Lois, as one can imagine, was indeed having a very hard time. She required two hospitalizations at the Boston Center for Children and was unable to leave Ms. Moffit's side, unable to share her with anyone, and unable to control her aggressive behavior. Her treating doctor diagnosed post-traumatic stress disorder. Once the adoptive mother had been found, Lois needed further inpatient care to help her adjust to leaving Ms. Moffit's home.

On January 14, 1995, Lois was discharged directly to the care of her newly-found adoptive mother. They had met a few times and seemed comfortable with each other. This woman, Faith Blackheart, was multi-racial (black and Indian), single, and childless. She was eager to adopt a child and to provide an environment that would satisfy Lois' need to be the sole focus. The adoption was finalized on January 30, 1996.

After visiting Lois several times, I concluded that she was adjusting to her new life. She attended school, participated in some after-school activities, was in frequent phone contact with Mary, and, above all, was receiving weekly therapy.

Approximately one year later, the department and I learned that Ms. Blackheart had moved with Lois to Washington, D.C., to be near her extended family. Contact stopped. From time to time, Lois and Mary phoned each other. After two years elapsed, Mary told me that Lois was phoning from a group foster care home in Florida. Although horrified to learn of this, there was nothing that I nor anyone in the Massachusetts DSS could do.

What was DSS' responsibility in the Broder case and how did the department discharge it? To begin, DSS was not responsible for the horrendous early family experiences inflicted on the girls by the drug-addicted mother and sadistic boyfriend. And, at the end of the story, Massachusetts DSS was not responsible for the apparent failure of the adoptive mother and Lois' dismal placement in a foster home in Florida. In between, the department was responsible for a great deal.

DSS knew from the outset that the Broder case involved two very young girls, one of whom had already suffered physical and sexual abuse, and both of whom had already been kicked out of the house by a family member. Their obligation was to look carefully at the foster-care placement they were going to find for them. In this instance, they had to go beyond guidelines of placement policy. That policy includes trying to find foster parents of similar racial background who live in a familiar neighborhood. Sometimes these criteria are useful in keeping a child his or her school and in touch with friends. In this case, neither priority applied. A department that was thinking of children's needs would have made locating foster parents who could offer genuine nurturing their first priority. Instead, based on the flimsiest possible examination, the DSS brought these two girls to a dreadful placement and did not even remove them when it learned four months later about there were very unsavory aspects of this residence. Alice Grasso's interest was not piqued when she took Mary to the hospital for vaginal bleeding. Remember, the girls were not removed from this placement because the department learned they were subjected to vicious sexual assault, but because the foster mother informed the worker that she had to close the home.

Return for a moment to their worker, Alice Grasso. *She was unable to learn the vitally important information that the girls willingly told their next foster mother within one month of placement. They openly spoke of their experience to the district attorney. Was Grasso willfully blind and deaf?*

This outrageous unwillingness to carefully examine homes for appropriate placement only got worse. Lois, reeling from her last experience with the Hoppers, and losing the companionship of her sister—not always friendly, but familiar—was placed in a foster home with a woman who spoke a different language, and who, on superficial examination, revealed very little knowledge about children. When the school attempted to phone the social worker with concerns about Lois, the worker, supervisor, and administrator did not return phone calls and were initially reluctant to hear that the child was once again in dire straits. Between 1986, when the case opened, and 1993, when the much-delayed termination trial took place, the case had no observable supervision or management. This was a social service agency that had lost sight of its goal of protecting children. It had substituted a series of formalized behaviors meant to give the impression that they offered protection, when, in fact, they offered nothing of the kind.

Case 2: The Perez Children

Children:	Carlita Perez	Date of birth: June 14, 1990
	Juanda Perez	Date of birth: June 19, 1991
	Rosie Perez	Date of birth: May 23, 1992
	Joa Perez	Date of birth: June 11, 1993

Mother:	Irene Provitch	
Father:	Juan Perez	

Race:	Czech-Hispanic

I was the attorney for the father, Juan Perez.

In December 1992, a DSS investigator and a police officer responded to a call from a neighbor regarding three children who were crying a lot in the

Perez apartment next door. The police and the department arrived to find the children alone. Their mother, Irene Provitch, returned shortly, explaining that she had to go out and thought a neighbor was watching them. The three very small girls were not dressed properly for the cold December night, the apartment was in disarray, and the mother appeared to be completely overwhelmed. Ms. Provitch's native language was Czech. She spoke English poorly, but managed to communicate that she did not have enough money for the next day's food, and she did not know where the father was or when he would return.

The social worker brought the three girls, Carlita, Juanda, and Rosie, to Boston Children's Hospital for evaluation. The evaluation team learned from the mother that all three children had been born prematurely. Eventually it became clear that they had suffered serious developmental delays. One child, Rosie, was retarded, and another, Juanda, had some cerebral palsy. The mother admitted to being overwhelmed and depressed, and expressed relief when told that the department was going to place the children in temporary foster care.

One month later, the father, Juan Perez, returned from Florida, where he had been looking for work. He had recently been laid off from his job as an electrician's assistant and thought that perhaps he could find work in Florida. Mr. Perez had told Ms. Provitch where he was going, why, and when he would return. She appeared not to have understood him.

Shortly after his return home he discovered that the children were taken by DSS. He phoned the department office and arranged for weekly visits of the children with him in their home. The visits went well. Despite his new job, Mr. Perez was able to be home when the girls were brought for a visit. The worker who brought the children observed that the mother had a flat emotional affect and seemed indifferent to the girls. Mr. Perez was warm and affectionate. The girls were happy to see him.

Mr. Perez never really understood, and the department never really explained to him, that the government of Massachusetts had the right to remove the children permanently from his care if their home situation did not improve. Nor did he fully understand the importance of their next set of instructions, that Ms. Provitch *must* allow a parental aid into the house to teach her how to care for the children. He did not force the children's mother to allow this because he knew she would not permit it. She had always refused help; he assumed that was her right, and he did not grasp the depth of the girls' problems. Mr. Perez later explained to me that his conversational English was poor because when he arrived in this country from Guatemala, he enrolled in a technical training program and learned, primarily, technical English; he was much less adept at "everyday" English. The department made no attempt communicate to him in Spanish and refused to concede that he was, therefore, confused about many things, including the time of his scheduled visits with the girls.

The department's attitude toward Mr. Perez was problematic from the start. The first they knew of him, he had "abandoned" his family for a month during the winter. To do what? They did not know. And they did not know that he was planning to return. When he returned he was treated as *persona non grata* by everyone connected with the case. The court investigator, who herself was Spanish-speaking, had ample time to interview him in person after he returned to Boston. But she satisfied herself with spending five minutes on the telephone. Her report dwelt more on his absence than on his responsible attitude toward making money for his family. When I asked the Children's Hospital evaluators whether they could envision a place for the father in their children's lives, they were horrified. Even though they had not met him, they had already concluded that he was one of those amoral men who brought children into the world and then abandoned them.

This problem was enormously exacerbated by the anti-father bias that pervades the department, and the particular anti-father animus of the department attorney for this case, Nancy Dirk. She was contemptuous of anyone who expressed a favorable view toward fathers, and communicated her distaste to the social workers under her supervision. I attempted to explain that Mr. Perez was genuinely unaware of his children's developmental problems. While he could be faulted for that, he was kind and loving and eager to work with the department to do what was best for his girls. Attorney Dirk responded scathingly to these entreaties. She chose to ignore the foster-care reviews, which commented on his attention to and concern for his children, and the evaluating psychologist who wrote, "Mr. Perez does genuinely care for the children. He has a warmth and concern that he can express." Attorney Dirk was not interested in Mr. Perez' qualities, because she had determined *a priori* that Mr. Perez' fatherhood rights to the three girls should be terminated and that he should lose them permanently. She began to make jokes about how the department was going to "get that little boy of his."

A son, Joa, was born on June 11, 1993. The pregnancy was full term and the baby was normal. It had been six months since the girls were placed in foster care. The department had found good foster care for them, with Spanish-speaking families in the neighborhood. The department was beginning to suggest that their goal for these children was not reunification, but permanent custody leading to adoption. Because Mr. Perez finally understood that Ms. Provitch's refusal to learn how to care for a child could cost him permanent custody of his three daughters and would jeopardize his ability to keep his son with him, he cooperated with the department in arranging full-time day care during his working hours, and promised to take care of Joa when he was not working. He convinced Ms. Provitch that she should simply absent herself from the apartment. Since she had found a job to her liking, and did not like her apartment or childcare, she was happy to absent herself. Mr. Perez performed his tasks well. The department kept very careful watch.

What Mr. Perez finally understood, to his everlasting anguish, was that when the department took "permanent custody" it was the beginning of a one-way trip down a road that was very hard to reverse, that he could reach a point where he would never see his daughters again. Since the three pre-adoptive families lived in the same area, and since they were all Spanish-speaking, I asked the department to consider an open adoption. An open adoption allows for specific, limited contact between the biological parent and the adopted child. The plan can only be put in place if the adopting parents and the biological parents really understand its limits and agree to its terms. I felt that Mr. Perez would be a perfect candidate for this, and that if DSS would explain to the adopting parents how the open adoption worked, they would consider it. DSS would not consider my request.

Mr. Perez continued to spend all his free time with Joa. As Joa approached age three he became increasingly unruly. DSS decided that Mr. Perez needed instruction in child management. For four months a parent-aide visited the home weekly, teaching Mr. Perez meal-planning, limit-setting, and safety measures. The aide wrote in her final report that Joa was a very active three-year-old, and that "Mr. Perez has taken good care of Joa and appears to be very nurturing." All of this activity took place when Ms. Provitch was at work, some distance from the house.

In early 1996, DSS assigned Stacy Gallows to replace Attorney Dirk, who was leaving the agency. Attorney Dirk informed Ms. Gallows that "this family does not allow parent-aides in the house." Attorney Gallows had the parent-aide report, whose findings I just quoted sitting in her files. Nonetheless, she reported to the court that that Mr. Perez did not cooperate with DSS. I proceeded to show the report to the judge and to read from it. Attorney Gallows did not change her position.

A week after the parent-aide filed her report, Joa's day-care center informed DSS that he had bruises on his legs and arms. In response to the department's 51A, Mr. Perez explained Joa ran very fast and tripped a lot. On the previous Sunday morning, while he and other fathers were playing with their children, Joa had fallen. During the course of the questioning, the investigating worker learned that Ms. Provitch had occasionally been alone with Joa when Mr. Perez' work schedule prevented him from being present, but Joa was not yet picked up for day care, or he was already returned from day care. She was already under suspicion because DSS said it saw thumb-sized black-and-blue marks on Joa's legs, suggesting that Ms. Provitch had restrained him too vigorously (to keep him from running and falling down?).

Sensing trouble for Mr. Perez, I obtained letters from the fathers who had been with Mr. Perez in the playground on that Sunday morning. The letters explained that they had been with Mr. Perez many Sundays on that playground. All the little boys ran and fell a lot. They also thought Mr. Perez spent more time with his son than most fathers, and was very good to him. I further suggested to the department that Ms. Provitch could not seriously harm Joa if she cared for him during an occasional half-hour in the morning or afternoon. I explained that this was necessitated by the demands of Mr. Perez' work. Attorney Gallows replied, "Tell him to quit his job."

Efforts to bring some perspective into the department's thinking were to no avail. The department filed a care-and-protection petition against Mr. Perez, alleging abuse and neglect, and told him to come to court. He knew from past experience that the agency had already built an impregnable wall against him.

Fearing that he would lose his son as he had lost his daughters, and knowing what a frightening experience it would be for Joa to be placed with strangers, he packed his son and his belongings into a rented truck and fled Massachusetts. He left behind his friends, a good job, the city where his daughters lived, and all hope of ever seeing them again.

What were the department's responsibilities in this case?

The department could not transform the girls' mother into a good caretaker. It could not erase the consequences of their premature births and subsequent neglect. However, the department could have prevented the bitter end to this tragedy had it not reduced Mr. Perez to a stereotype. By refusing to acknowledge him as an individual, and by not granting him his humanity, they brought needless fear and profound sorrow into his life, and they *permanently* severed a relationship between three children and their biological father. They were willing, in fact, anxious, to remove a very young boy from his father's love and care and place him with strangers in order to prove a point about fathers.

Joa was not the only child whose well-being the department threatened. Three little girls will grow up with no knowledge of who their father was. They will not know that he loved them. The adopting parents appeared to be kind, very simple people, people who would not consider it to be their job to offer answers or guidance to a child asking about her origins.

Once DSS had decided the children would be removed permanently, there was no avenue of redress. When the girls were first removed, Mr. Perez was given weekly visits with them in his home. They played together and sometimes prepared a meal. But the social worker handling his case left the agency. Her replacement decided to stop bringing the girls to Mr. Perez' house. The department, under the baleful eye of Attorney Dirk, began to reduce visits and insist that they take place in the social work office (an unfriendly environment). I protested the reduced visits. Among other things, it is against DSS' own policy to reduce visits without court permission. But once Attorney Dirk had decided to reduce visits, "policy" was useless. There was no way to appeal her decision. The less he saw the girls, the less they thought of him as their father. He was losing them even before the court severed ties.

There are many reasons why DSS is treated with disrespect in the poorer communities of Boston. Mr. Perez was a popular man in his working-class East Boston neighborhood. When he left with Joa, every one of his neighbors knew what DSS was doing to him, and why, and they hated the agency for it. The department's mandate is to protect children from family abuse. In this neighborhood, families believe that they need an agency to protect them from DSS abuse. DSS has to understand that it cannot offer "protection" to people in whom it has incited fear and loathing.

Case 3: The Daniels Children

Children:	Justin Daniels	Date of birth: May 3, 1987
	Janet Daniels	Date of birth: March 22, 1990
	Jack, Jr.	Date of birth: August 12, 1991

| *Mother:* | Evelyn Daniels |
| *Father:* | John Daniels |

| Race: | White Anglo-Saxon-Irish |

When I asked my colleagues to share their case files with me, there were many offers. I chose this one, including a summary by the court investigator, because it best expresses the frustration of those who work as attorneys representing the families whom DSS brings to court on care-and-protection petitions. It concerns a deeply dysfunctional family. In this case the mother of the children had been in foster care most of her childhood, as were her four siblings. The father had four other children. He was an alcoholic. He had a criminal record that included violence, and clearly had abused his children. The Daniels family came to the attention of the Boston Juvenile Court in July 1993 as the result of a care-and-protection petition based on allegations of sexual abuse by the father and neglect by the mother, as well as domestic violence and substance abuse in the home. While there was no concrete evidence to support the allegations of sexual abuse, there was substantial information to support allegations of domestic violence and chronic alcoholism by father. There was some reason to believe that Ms. Daniels was colluding with Mr. Daniels in allowing contact with the children against the orders of the court. This resulted in the children being removed from her care in January 1994. At that time, the children presented with difficult behavior. Placement appeared necessary and appropriate. "Unfortunately," the court investigator wrote, "what happened to these children when they were removed from the care of their mother is simply unbelievable." In his 1995 report to the court, he wrote as follows,

> Justin has been placed in a series of totally inappropriate foster homes, which ultimately resulted in his hospitalization at age seven for suicidal, out-of-control behavior. He is now placed in a long-term residential facility, where he will need placement for at least a year. Janet was moved from a foster home where she had apparently been doing well to a foster home which the department had prior indication would be inappropriate for the child. As predicted, her second placement disrupted within several weeks and Janet was placed in a series of inappropriate homes until she also needed psychiatric intervention, hospitalization, and finally specialized foster care. Jack Jr. has fared somewhat better than his siblings, as he has only had a handful of foster-home placements in the last year. He reportedly had made a good adjustment to his first foster home when the department inexplicably decided to move him to the home that was reported to be

inappropriate for his sister. The placement was disrupted and Jack Jr. was placed in his current foster home, where he has remained since August 1994. While his home has provided physical stability for Jack Jr., there are serious concerns for the lack of nurturance and emotional support. This is a home where this three-year-old boy, reportedly traumatized by the chaos and domestic violence in his parent's home, is forced and encouraged to defend himself against the attacks of another child. The fact that this foster mother would only take Jack Jr. into her home if she could send him to full-day daycare raises questions about how welcome this child is in his home. Fortunately, Jack Jr. appears to be significantly connected to his day-care teacher and his therapist at school.

It seems evident that Justin, Janet, and Jack Jr. have not been well served by the department's intervention. What is curious is that *the department represents that all of the children's problems are a result of traumatic experiences which occurred while in the care of the parents. The department does not acknowledge that the children's experiences in foster care have been contributing factors to their current dysfunction.* During the first few months of placement the children visited regularly with their parents and apparently were not exhibiting the extreme behaviors which they would later demonstrate. *These extreme behaviors only appeared with the onset of multiple inappropriate placements. Information available suggests that Justin experienced significant trauma as the result of the physical and emotional abuse at the hands of his second foster family.*

The two younger children were reunited with their mother in 1997; Justin joined them one year later, in 1998. Justin continued in day treatment for the next year. In 1999, the three children and their mother lost their apartment. They moved into the Cambridge, MA, YWCA, which maintains living space for homeless women and their children. At their attorney's last visit, they seemed to have "turned the corner." "They will never be without awful memories and anger," she said, "but the children appear to understand that their future looks better than their past. It might even look good." He might have said, "It might even look good in spite of the Department of Social Services."

The Massachusetts Campaign for Children and Youth (MCCY), the very organization that sued DSS for the size of its social-worker caseload in 1980, released a report in January 1999. It said that few abused or neglected children made it into the DSS caseload the first time someone called in a complaint, that the agency required at the minimum a second phone call. MCCY charged DSS with turning away 75% of the cases that came before it without offering any services.

The unsatisfactory response to phone calls has always been a problem for callers to the department. An example surfaced in the press just as this book was being completed. The *Boston Globe* reported that school officials had tried to reach DSS on thirteen different occasions to tell them about five children in one family who were obviously being seriously neglected. Their phone calls were never returned. Subsequently, a neighbor of the Harden family called the police to report that the father was beating his wife. The police found the children, aged twenty-two months to thirteen years, shoeless and clad only in pajamas. The month was January. The apartment reeked of rotten food and garbage, cat and dog feces were everywhere, and the baby's crib was filled with empty beer cans and roaches. The most distressing aspect of this was that the family was known to DSS. According to the DSS spokeswoman, a worker had visited the family a mere one month previous to this discovery, but she did not think the situation warranted removal of the children. The response of the state administration was typical: the governor fired the worker. A vice-president of the Social Workers Union lamented that things like this happen because social workers caseloads are too large.

This sounds like a weak and almost irrelevant defense. Yet, it is clearly part of the problem. More accurately, the union official might have said, "The social worker has far too many things to do in one day, or one week, including too many cases to attend to."

There are many, many reasons why the front-line social worker makes horrendous judgments. A profile of the typical social worker would reveal that she is a recent graduate from college and has taken only a couple of psychology courses. Her intentions are good. Her entire experience with family dynamics is with her own family, which is usually some variety of middle class. Regardless of her social background, she has never met people as dysfunctional as the ones she's meeting in the course of her work. She does not feel safe in the inner city. The pay has always been poor, and she gets limited training and support from the department. The demands of her job are overwhelming, simply in terms of the hours required. The Mahoney Report calculated that a social worker would have to work twelve hours a day to be caught up at the end of each week. Were we to pick a typical day at random, it might look like this: The social worker picks up the client's kids at their foster home and drives them to the DSS office for their mandated visit with their mother. The worker observes the one-hour visit and then returns them to foster care. Are there several children from one family in different placements? If so, there are several different pick-ups and returns. The worker must also make regular check-up visits to children in placement. The more troubled children might be placed in residential treatment centers, often more than an hour's drive from the Boston offices.

Is it a court day? Social workers are required to be present in court for the hearings of their cases *despite the fact that they are not queried, nor permitted to address the court;* only the DSS lawyer is supposed to present the DSS case in court. This is an inexcusable abuse of a social worker's time. If the worker is in the courthouse all day waiting for her case to be called, she is not managing her practice nor returning phone calls. The Boston Juvenile Court social workers' office, which serves department needs in the courthouse, has only two phones for the use of the twenty or more workers who may need it on a given day. Fortunately for the modern-day social worker, wireless phones are ubiquitous and cheap. But a day spent in court is a day that the worker is not recording her case notes, not helping clients find needed services, not picking up children for visitation. The social worker spends all her time trying to catch up. What if there is a call for an emergency placement? The monthly count for new entries into the department's system, statewide, is 750 children. Surely there will be numerous emergencies within that group. Any catch-up time that might have been available will be absorbed by an emergency. It is no wonder that over half of the newly-hired workers quit in their first year.

Sympathy for the on-line worker, however, does not diminish the conclusion that DSS has a profoundly troubling habit of allowing the outrageous behavior of some workers to continue unchecked.

By an uncanny coincidence, as I was concluding the writing of this chapter, a physician-colleague of my own doctor, aware of my interests and this book, telephoned me. She wanted to communicate her outrage concerning the following story.

Nancy lives in a pleasant suburb of Boston. Her husband is a research scientist; she is a physician. They have two children, Brad and Laura. The story concerns Laura and her friend Gail, both sixth-grade students at the local public school. Gail had been in the legal custody of her maternal grandmother all of her life because her mother had been diagnosed as having a psychological disorder that made it impossible for her to be the primary caretaker for her daughter (a borderline personality mixed with depression.) Unfortunately, in the middle of this past school year, Gail's grandmother succumbed to cancer. Her mother, Molly, tried to take over, but in her own confusion and depression, she began preventing Gail from attending school. In February 2000, the school, honoring its obligation to report truancy to DSS, called the department. The department filed a CHINS petition in court (Child In Need of Services, used to bring truant pre-teens or teens into court to be scolded and tracked by probation). Without notifying the school or learning of the mothers of school friends who had always been involved in Gail's care, DSS placed Gail in a Spanish-speaking foster home forty-five minutes from her community. They told her she couldn't contact any of her friends because she needed to adjust to her new environment.

School personnel and the mothers of Gail's friends began to make frantic phone calls to DSS to nullify this removal. DSS did not return their calls. When the case came into court for its scheduled review in March, the mothers, and a lawyer privately hired for Gail's mother, convinced the judge that Gail should be returned instantly to her community and her school. They further argued that DSS should do an emergency home study of the home of one of her friends, where she would live temporarily.

Anna, the temporary foster mother with whom Gail had been living, began searching for a home where Gail could live for an extended period of time, and perhaps be adopted. She asked DSS for help. The supervisor replied that DSS could not help because it had no data on foster care in this particular community. It isn't clear why she said this, because it was known that the area office had a great deal of information about foster homes. By posting her own notices and making inquiries, Anna learned of available homes. She also got good advice: when having difficulty with the worker or the supervisor, go directly to the top, go to the area director.

This advice proved very useful when summer came. Gail was enjoying herself in a camp that Anna had found and paid for. During the last week of camp, a DSS supervisor contacted the head counselor at camp to inform her that on Thursday she was coming to remove Gail from camp in order to place her in a home for troubled teens! Again, as when Gail had been summarily removed from school, the supervisor told no one of this plan, including Gail's court-assigned lawyer. The head counselor said, "You are telling me that you want to remove her the day just before the last day, when we give out the awards; she is receiving some awards. I will not allow you to remove her." She alerted the two foster mothers and they, along with the friend who called me with the story, started making the usual frantic phone calls, eventually reaching the area director. He overrode the decision of this thoroughly-discredited supervisor.

The reader should consider this: *the three women making the phone calls had twenty years of postgraduate education among them. Would a barely literate, easily-intimidated single mother have had a scintilla of a chance in getting the supervisor's plan reversed?* It is *critical*, if DSS is going to survive as an independent child-protection agency, that it be aware of a worker or supervisor whose judgments are harmful and re-direct that person, or or see to it that the person is fired. It is entirely unacceptable that a correct outcome of a case must depend on community members willing and able to invest hours in making phone calls.

There have been decided improvements in DSS' performance since federal money (ASFA again) became available in 1997. Several new evaluations published in 1998–1999 reported favorably on the department's efforts to reduce the caseload of most social workers (though not consistently in "crisis cities"). There are other favorable developments: The Department has implemented a several-step, several-day training program for new workers—a clear improvement over the previous practice of handing new social workers a huge caseload on their first day, offering some encouraging words and little else. Federal money has been put to excellent use with the installation of a $50-million automated case-management system. Readers already know that federal money has also been used to expand the DSS adoption division. Together with a new juvenile court mandate to reduce the amount of time children are in placement without resolution, children waiting to be adopted can now expect a shorter waiting time to be legally freed for adoption.

Several new, promising programs have begun. One is called Patch; the word is used to mean "neighborhood" in England, which is where the Patch idea originated. The English model assigns staff to cover specific "patches," or neighborhoods. The primary goals of "patchworking" are to remove barriers to service integration and to deliver services at the neighborhood level by linking DSS workers to formal and informal resources. Boston's Patch program has been in the planning stages for and only recently (winter 2000) opened its doors. The social worker who brought it to the United States, Frederico Bird, first observed it in England, then brought it to Iowa, his next place of employment, and thence to Boston. The Boston Patch program has been opened in a busy neighborhood community center. It provides the space for meetings and activities. DSS and many other community agencies, such as the Department of Youth Services, Healthy Babies, and Family Services, participate.[18] But it is the local residents and owners of the local businesses who are the heart of the Patch project. Corinne Coltorino, an administrator of one of Boston's six divisional DSS

---

[18] Massachusetts copied the popular Health Baby program from Hawaii. It offers a home visitor/nurse to every first-time mother under the age of twenty-one. The mother gets good advice and some companionship. The program also saves the Commonwealth money: If a mother asks a nurse to come to her house because the baby is teething and has a fever, it costs the state $35. If the mother takes her feverish child to a hospital emergency room, the answer to her question about the cause of the fever will cost the state $300.

offices, whose energy brought the Boston program to life, hopes social workers and the neighborhood will get to know and trust each other. She believes that if the workers know the people in the community, they will not make so many errors in judgment in the initial stages of their cases, and that the families will be less frightened of the agency and will ask for help if they need it.

The Mahoney Report urged DSS to join with other agencies in order to share information and keep each agency aware of what the other was doing. However, the Civil Liberties Union contends that information-sharing violates the privacy rights of the child, and opposes inter-agency meetings about a specific person. This is an important issue that needs further examination by both sides.

Also, DSS has joined with the Department of Education to create the School and Community Support Project. This program, begun a few years ago, now operates in nineteen communities. The program was desperately needed; with luck, it will gain more support and spread to every community in Massachusetts. It recognizes that children in foster care bring their needs and experiences into the classroom. The project provides support services for the children, the teachers and the foster parents who are new to the foster care system. As with the inter-agency meeting described above, the need for confidentiality can get in the way of the relay of useful information. DSS and the School Department have to write a set of guidelines that detail what can and cannot be revealed. These communication problems, however, are not insuperable and can be dealt with. The important point is that children in foster care are usually cast adrift to fend for themselves. Any program that offers them support should be enthusiastically applauded.

Another Mahoney recommendation has been fulfilled. The report called on DSS to clarify its goals. It said, "The policy of the Commonwealth should be redefined to eliminate potential ambiguity or conflict between the goals of protecting children and preserving families." State law and DSS policy have indeed clarified the goals; child protection comes first. Where the best interests of children conflict with the rights of parents, the children's needs will determine the outcome of the case. As I suggested in the chapter on parents' rights, advocates for parents decry this reversal of priorities. Perhaps in a more ideal world, resources would be available that would enable children's welfare and parents' rights to have equal weight. But we do not live in an ideal world, and the risk of harm to children is too overwhelming. At this point, neglected and abused children would benefit more from improved foster care than from more in-home services to dysfunctional families.

Other goals listed in the Mahoney Report, however, remain unfulfilled. The commission criticized the agency for the haphazard methods used in opening cases. It pointed out that the initial judgment brought to a case is the critical judgment for all the remaining time that a case is in DSS custody. The authors recommend a multi-track assessment model that differentiates low risk, moderate risk and serious cases and provides clear treatment or legal paths for each. The *Boston Globe* editorialized, "It's a good preventive model that deserves a long, sympathetic look from DSS." As of this writing, there is no indication the DSS is moving on this recommendation.

Mahoney commission members were highly critical of fair hearing procedures, noting infrequent scheduling, lack of due process, and use of untrained personnel. The Fair Hearing statute is supposed to be one of the "failsafe" procedures that the legislature and DSS cite to prove that fairness prevails; i.e., "You can always request a review for a decision you don't like at a Fair Hearing." As an attorney, this is my experience with the Fair Hearing process: I had a client who requested a Fair Hearing. I wrote to the correct office and was assigned a date one month hence. Then my client changed his mind, so I began to write the letter canceling the date, when I noticed that it was actually *one year and one month hence!* I concluded, along with the commission report, that this right of review was an item of DSS chicanery.

Other failures persist that are far more important to children's well-being than a weak Fair Hearing process. The quality of foster care remains abysmally poor. Children continue to be placed in overcrowded, inappropriate homes. Perhaps the most vexing of all failures is the failure to build careful review into the structure of case management. This kind of review requires a more competent, activist supervisory staff than the Boston area DSS currently employs.

In summary, DSS is a powerful agency whose behavior is idiosyncratic, whose decisions are virtually closed to review, and which often inflicts harm on the children in its custody. The avenues of review, as I indicated, are useless. The department, as an institution, will not return phone calls and will not allow attorneys to meet with department representatives to try to put a case into a different posture. They respond to every question as though it were a challenge to their very existence. They close ranks and lock themselves into a position long after all other parties can see the harm the position is causing a family. There is no genuine fair hearing process; there is an ombudsman, but he exists largely to listen to complaints and explain the actions of DSS, not to question those actions. Juvenile court judges seldom directly challenge a DSS position. Unfortunately, the Massachusetts Supreme Judicial Court has reinforced this judicial reluctance by issuing two decisions clearly implying that the juvenile courts should give great weight to the decisions of the department.

The problems of the department have remained unchanged for twenty years, despite going through four DSS Commissioners and receiving a large infusion of federal money to put towards innovative programs. What can be done?

I conducted more than a dozen interviews in several states, from former top-management to former DSS attorneys to current long-time social workers. The consensus is that the supervisory level fails in its job. People are promoted to supervisors on the basis of their years of service, not their competence; their union sees to it that they will never be dismissed. Therefore, competence is random, not routine.

Those who have studied the problem of social service agencies have suggested some solutions. One possibility divides agency tasks into different divisions with different leadership. Law enforcement would be one division. It would perform the job of initial investigation. Courts would be another division; they would monitor foster care. DSS would remain in charge of providing services. I do not think this is a workable solution. Police cannot be social workers (although I acknowledge they are often asked to be), and should not be making social-worker decisions about neglect. I would only support the courts' monitoring of foster care if they were part of an integrated family court structure such as I proposed in the last chapter. Recall that I advocated a family court that places the department under the aegis of a Chief Judge. However, if Massachusetts were to do this, *two* firmly entrenched institutions would have to change: the Massachusetts court system (over 350 years old) and the Department of Social Services (only forty years old, but rigid). I do not believe the will for this exists. Therefore, I am not recommending it.

It is critical that Massachusetts DSS be overseen by an agency with muscle. After a thorough review of the literature and many interviews, I have come to the conclusion that the Massachusetts legislature should create an Office of Child Advocate (OCA), modeled on that of Rhode Island.

In the aftermath of a series of child deaths similar to the one in Massachusetts' Denise Gallison case, Rhode Island created an oversight agency. The Rhode Island OCA is a state agency under the executive branch. It is staffed entirely by attorneys, social workers, investigators and advocates who are employees of the OCA[19]. By statute, it has full subpoena powers and access to confidential records. It is charged with a periodic review of the Rhode Island Department of Children, Youth, and Family Services (DCYF), which is Rhode Island's DSS. With this mandate, it regularly reviews DCYF procedures, policies, and cases, and conducts annual site visits of all placements, including residential placements. It reviews all complaints that come before it and investigates those where "it appears that a child may be in need of assistance from the child advocate." And it reviews orders of the family court relating to juveniles with the power to request reviews as "required by the best interests of the child." (Compare this to the extremely weak MA ombudsman and the close-to-non-existent Fair Hearing Review.)

The OCA also sits on the General Assembly's Children's Code Commission, which reviews all children's legislation and routinely initiates or testifies on behalf of legislative proposals affecting children. Many recommendations made by the OCA have been implemented by DCYF and/or enacted into law by the General Assembly.

According to the American Bar Association for Children and the Law, the Rhode Island OCA has been the model ombudsman office. Connecticut, Delaware, and Georgia have copied it. Lawsuits and *Boston Globe* headlines are —not the best way to call the department to account. An Office for Children Advocate is. The 1995 Senate Report on Foster Care hinted at something like

---

[19] The virtue of a staff attorney, as opposed to a private attorney, is that a staff attorney does not have an outside practice that commands his time and attention. There is no problem maintaining court dates.

the OCA when it recommended an Independent Children's Services Commission.

DSS should welcome this agency. A Massachusetts law school professor and child advocate working in Rhode Island when the OCA was created told me that there were enough judges, legislators, and child advocates actively in favor a strong child advocate office to ensure that the legislation passed without difficulty. "After all," he said, "it's hard to argue against an agency that is entirely child-focused." However, as we brought the conversation back to Massachusetts, we agreed, ruefully, that the Massachusetts DSS would not accept oversight gracefully. A fight by organized child advocates working with the legislature would be necessary. It is a fight that would be well worth it.

Massachusetts children have been consigned to almshouses, indentured to brutish masters, overworked in cotton mills, and adjudged competent to stand trial for misdemeanors or crimes from the age of seven. The first protection of abused children emerged from an agency dedicated to the preservation of animals. Now the public appears to be offering "protection" from an agency that is as likely to hurt them as to help them.

Supreme Court Justice William J. Brennan wrote, "No society can assure its children that there will be no unhappy families. It can tell, them, however, that their government will not be allowed to contribute to their pain." (*Bowen v. Gillard*, 1987)

Massachusetts' protection of its children is long overdue.

Personal Note

After doing the research for this book, I came away angrier than I had been previously about the 350 years of the underclass in America. I knew the Puritans did not have a lot of sympathy for slackers, but I did not understand that their proof-of-faith *required* that a poor population live among them. I had not realized how strenuously the clergy and their followers clung to the belief that money served a salutary purpose in *their* pockets but would only corrupt people who didn't have any. Although the opening chapters revealed many sanctimonious gems, my favorite was Reverend William Ellery Channing's sermon in which he claimed that death from starvation was better than death caused by overeating, that shivering in the freezing cold was better than "our daughters…(being brought to death)…by their rich attire," and that the overworked were better off than the rich because they were not bored.

Given this unpromising history, I suppose I should feel satisfaction in how far we've come. I acknowledge that we have come a long way, but not far enough. I cite, for example, health care.

I am more contemptuous than I was previously toward the American Medical Association and American College of Pediatricians, whose blind greed led them to fulminate against national health care and clinics for women and children. I had never imagined that United States Senators could produce the insane rhetoric that characterized the debate on the creation of the Children's Bureau. It made me appreciate more than ever before the bravery of the settlement house women who led the fight, because if Congress was willing to speak about them in such scathing terms, I know for certain that the rest of the country was even more vituperative.

I also want to say that in the course of doing my research I became so enamoured of Jane Addams, Sophinisba Breckenridge, Julia Lathrop, Florence Kelly, Lillian Wald, Dr. Alice Hamilton, Frances Perkins—all settlement house women—that if I ever write another book, it will be about them.

I searched for leaders who inspire, who have vision in every nook and cranny of our modern American life. I could not find them. I certainly could not find them in the Massachusetts Department of Social Services. A more scared agency, with less vision, cannot be imagined. I am well aware of the limited impact that a social service agency can have on the lives of the underclass. But they owe it to the children to try. When I first started working at the Boston Juvenile Court, I noticed how consistently the social workers disregarded the emotional needs of the children. They seemed not to notice that virtually everything the department did, except when it was removing a child from immediate danger, was done in a manner guaranteed to further upset and not soothe the child. I thought this was because the workers were too young to have children of their own—as a result they did not know what the emotional needs of children in a typical DSS situation were. Then I noticed several things: attorneys manage the DSS cases, not social workers, because it is the attorneys who bring the cases to court. Their attitudes have a strong, but unacknowledged, influence. In the Boston-area offices, where my cases originated, almost all the attorneys were young mothers with young children. Their attitude toward DSS children was even more dismissive than that of the social workers. Here was the best example I knew of where the humanity of the client was missing from the equation. I felt confident that they would be horrified if their children were dealt with as though they were just one more piece of furniture that had to be moved. Yet that is how the children in DSS custody are treated. It would not be difficult, and it would not cost a lot of money, to train workers and attorneys to respect the emotional needs of the children in their care.

As for all the other DSS policy, much of it is driven by the desperate need to prevent a screaming headline in the *Boston Globe*. This policy has little to do with what is best for the children or the family. The *Globe* has assigned itself the job of being a watchdog agency for DSS. DSS definitely needs a watchdog agency, but not one that sees bad agency practice as a chance to sell more newspapers. The exposés have occasionally helped DSS to become more responsible, but they also have the effect of paralyzing the department. The standard for decision becomes "the *Globe* must approve of this," not "This is best for these particular children."

Often times I feel as if my judgments are too quick. I know the parents in the DSS caseload are, more often than not, irresponsible. I know some of them lie about taking drugs, lie about why they missed scheduled visits, relapse after being clean, and, above all, do not seem to understand or care about the damage they are doing to their own children. So I can understand an overworked social worker saying to herself, "If she doesn't care, why should I?" Of course, that is exactly the reason the worker needs to care.

I keep thinking about the children. Two young teens, strangers to each other, having a desultory conversation in a DSS office late one afternoon while waiting for a worker to find them a placement. "I hope that this new foster mother, whoever she is, doesn't make Spanish rice."

"Oh yeah. I hate Spanish rice."

I thought, what a life these kids have! It's four p.m. They don't know where they are spending the night. How many foster homes have they been in before? Each home presents different foods, different rules. Are they allowed to say that they don't like a particular food? Are they worried that someone in this new placement will be nasty? Have they given up caring about it? How can a person concentrate on anything—especially school—in this situation? Can a person believe he or she will be really safe or live in one home for the remainder of their minor years? I think of the anger and generalized suspicion that these constant moves must engender. What a perfect recipe for producing a dysfunctional, or violent, adult.

A useful child-protection service would not merely react to crises. It would be proactive. It would be thinking about the whole of what the clients need: the right placements, adjustment to school, serious counseling about the constant loss all foster children experience. It would be in front of the state legislature telling the men and women what DSS kids need, shepherding the bills through the legislature. The city of Boston has six law schools and six colleges that have graduate schools of social work, social policy, or both. It should draw on the intellectual wealth of the surrounding community to help think through the larger issues of successful social-worker case management, client drug rehabilitation, better transportation, garbage removal, and street repair. Massachusetts' DSS is by no means the worst in the nation. It is in fact very good compared to many others. But it accepts low standards for itself. Last year the department announced, with obvious satisfaction, that there had been no deaths of children in DSS custody that year. This should be a starting goal for DSS, not an end goal.

I want to return to the national stage for a moment to say how interesting I found the Johnson-Nixon-Clinton anti-poverty programs. It seemed as though Johnson really believed in these programs. But he never lost sight of the fact that the liberal New York crowd would love them. He had a burning desire to be seen as more progressive than Kennedy, and therefore, be more adulated. Nixon appeared to be completely indifferent to the programs he sponsored, but he too, urged on by Daniel Patrick Moynihan, saw these generous programs as a way to get the East Coast liberal establishment—his lifelong enemy—to sit up and take notice. Clinton, who expressed endless feelings of pain for anyone and anything, appeared to produce the most Draconian of all possible welfare bills. Indeed, the people who lost benefits in the first months if the bill's passage were the very most needy and disenfranchised—the non-English-speaking elderly and the handicapped. Many welfare advocates thought Clinton had lost his mind. Fortunately, alert workers and lawyers involved with these newest victims of conservative backlash prevailed in court and their benefits were restored. But Clinton's reputation in the social services community took a decisive blow. In that light, I observed three things that occurred in the year after the 1996 Welfare Bill went into effect that are worth noting. First, Clinton prevailed on Congress to double the childcare budget. Small though it is, it is twice the size that it would have been without him. Second, in 1997, Congress released a large amount of money to the states to improve their adoption services and their courts. Clinton was very much behind these measures. I do not know how successful other states have been in using their adoption money. Massachusetts has put it to good use. The same could be said for court improvement, the results of which can be seen everywhere in Boston: new courthouses, more judges, a state legislature more responsive to children's needs. Thus, although the tangible evidence is dispersed and not easy to pinpoint, I think his efforts had a direct, positive effect on children's well-being.

Finally, there is the earned-income tax credit. In the *New York Times* of December 26, 2000, reporter Jason De Parle evaluated the situation of the working and non-working poor: "By far, Mr. Clinton's most significant legacy to the working poor is in a large program of wage subsidies with an opaque name, the earned-income tax credits. The details are complicated, but the bottom line is not: the program provides low-wage workers with annual cash bonuses of up to nearly $3,900. Workers must have children to fully qualify." De Parle said Clinton had worked this provision into every budget that he presented to Congress starting in 1993, and doubled the amount over the years so that by 1999 the government paid almost $30 billion dollars a year in wage supplements. This figure is nearly twice what the federal government spent on the old welfare program, Aid to Families with Dependent Children, even at its peak. The fact that he could establish these programs during a period when a conservative Congress dictated the legislative agenda reveals his remarkable political skills and, I think, more genuine concern than his critics give him credit for. There are some useful lessons here for social welfare advocates: examine every corner of the federal budget to see where harm or help are lurking. Do not assume that one (or even two) unwelcome programs can define a political leader.

After considering all of this, what remains is what I began with: the real job of the social welfare advocate is to put a human face on the poor. All else follows.

NOTES ON SOURCES

The following history texts provided the framework for my historical research:

Bailyn, Bernard et al. *The Great Republic.* Lexington, MA: D.C.: Heath and Company, 1977.

Blum, John et al. *The National Experience,* 3rd ed. New York: Harcourt Brace Jovanovich, 1973.

Current, Richard et al. *American History,* 5th ed. New York: Alfred A. Knopf, 1979.

Hofstadter, Richard et al. *The United States,* 4th ed. Englewood Cliffs, New Jersey: Prentice-Hall, 1976.

The following social welfare texts provided the framework for my social welfare research:

Axxin, June and Herman Levin. *Social Welfare,* 4th ed. New York: Longman, 1997.

Day, Phyllis J. *A New History of Social Welfare.* Englewood Cliffs, New Jersey: Prentice-Hall, 1989.

Trattner, Walter I. *From Poor Law to Welfare State,* 5th ed. New York: The Free Press, 1994.

Chapter One

For Chapter One and subsequent chapters, legislation is summarized from the statutes recorded in Massachusetts Acts and Resolves, sequentially numbered, beginning with volume 1 in 1628.

A wide-ranging discussion of children's rights in this and subsequent chapters can be found in

Hawes, James M. *The Children's Rights Movement.* Boston: Twayne Publishers, 1991.

_____. *Children in Urban Society.* New York: Oxford University Press, 1971.

The principle historian of almshouses is:

Rothman, David A. *The Discovery of the Asylum: Social Order and Disorder in the New Republic.* Boston: Little Brown, & Co., 1971.

Chapter Two

Economic details of working-class life can be found in:

Green, James R. and Hugh Carter Donahue. *Boston Workers: A Labor History.* Boston: Trustees of the Boston Public Library, 1979.

Early poverty, particularly Massachusetts poverty can be found in:

Folks. Homer. *The Care of Destitute, Neglected, and Delinquent Children.* New York: Macmillan Co., 1902.

Kelso, Robert W. *The History of Public Poor Relief in Massachusetts, 1620-1920.* Boston: Houghton Mifflin Co., 1922.

The William Ellery Channing quote is from Mendelsohn, Jack. *Channing, The Reluctant Radical.* Boston: Little Brown & Co., 1971.

The Congregational story is recorded by Starkey, Marion L. *The Congregational Way.* Garden City, New York: Doubleday, & Co., 1966.

Discussion in this chapter and Chapter Three of the evolving concepts of family law were taken from:

Zainaldin, Jamil S. "The Emergence of American Family Law." *Northwestern University Law Review* 73 (February 1979): 1038-1089.

For perceptions of children in this era, see Slater, Peter G. *Children in the New England Mind.* New Hartford, Connecticut: Archon Books, 1977.

Chapter Three

The thrust and threat of dynamic industrialism is described in:
Hofstadter, Richard. *The American Political Tradition.*
New York: Vintage Books, 1948.

A wonderful description of the Vanderbilts' Newport parties is part of
Cooke, Alistair. *America.* New York: Alfred A. Knopf, 1973.

The chronicle of "scientific" or "organized" charity can be found in:
Watson, Frank Dekker. *The Charity Organization Movement in the
United States.* New York: Macmillian Company, 1922.
Bremmer, Robert H. "Scientific Philanthropy, 1873-1893." *Social Science
Review 30* (June 1956): 168-173.

For material on Jane Addams and Hull House see Anne Firor Scott.
"Jane Addams, Urban Crusader." In Garraty, John A. ed., *Historical
Viewpoints* Volume II, N.Y.: Harper & Row, 1979.

The development of social work as a profession can be found in:
Bruno, Frank J. *Trends in Social Work, 1874-1956.* New York:
Columbia University, 1957.
Lubove, Ray. *The Emergence of Social Work as a Career, 1880-1930.*
Cambridge, Massachusetts: Harvard University Press, 1965.
Rich, Margaret E. *A Belief in People, A History of Family Social Work.*
New York: Family Service Association of America, 1956.
Richmond Mary E. *Friendly Visiting Among the Poor.*
New York: Macmillan, 1903.

For details of the history of child placement, such as Charles
Birtwell's experiment with a carefully supervised group home or
Charles Loring Brace and the Children's Aid Society, see Thurston,
Henry W.
The Dependent Child. New York: Columbia University Press, 1930.

For the history of the Massachusetts Society for the Prevention of Cruelty
to Children, see
Hubbard, Ray S. *Crusading For Children, 1878-1943.*

Anderson, Paul Gerard. "The Origin, Emergence, and Professional Recognition of Child Protection." *Social Service Review 63* (June 1989): 222-244.

Chapter Four

Progressives and their priorities are well described in Wiebe, Robert H. *The Search for Order, 1877-1920.* New York: Hill & Wang, 1967.

For growth and change in American charities, see Warner, Amos G. *American Charities.* New York: Thomas Y. Crowell & Co., 1919.

Poverty and children in the first quarter of the nineteenth century are studied in
Bremner, Robert H. *From the Depths.* New York: New York University Press, 1956.
Faulkner, Harold U. *The Quest for Social Justice, 1898-1914.* New York: Macmillan, 1931.
Hagedorn, James M. *Foresaking Our Children.* Chicago: Lake View Press, 1995.

For details of the Sheppard-Towner fight see Lemmons, Stanley J. "The Sheppard Towner Act: Progressivism in the 1920s." *Journal of American History* 55 (March, 1969): 176-186.

Judge Benjamin Barr Lindsey's life and contribution to the juvenile court movement are detailed in
Hawes, James M. *The Children's Rights Movement.* Boston: Twayne Publishers, 1991.
Larsen, Charles L. *The Good Fight, the Life and Times of Ben Lindsey.* Chicago: Quadrangle, 1972.
Slater, Peter G. Ben Lindsey and the Denver Juvenile Court.
American Quarterly 20 (Summer 1968): 211-223.

The early history of the juvenile courts is chronicled in two law review articles:
Fox, Sanford J. "Juvenile Justice Reform: An Historical Perspective." 22 *Stanford Law Review* (1970): 1187-1239.
Mack, Julian. "The Juvenile Court." 23 *Harvard Law Review* (1909).

Discussion of how probation changed the juvenile court can be found in Schlossman, Steven L. *Love and the American Delinquent.* Chicago: University of Chicago Press, 1977.

Continuing examination of children's and parents' rights in light of government expansion into this area is the subject of Tiffin, Susan. *In Whose Best Interest?* Westport Connecticut: Greenwood Press, 1982.

The problem with mothers' pensions administered by the juvenile court is examined by Pelton, Leroy H. *For Reasons of Poverty: A Critical Analysis of the Public Welfare System in the United States.* New York: Preager, 1989.

Placement questions and issues are studied in:
Hasci, Thomas A. *Second Home: Orphan Asylums and Poor Families in America.* Cambridge: Harvard University Press, 1997.
Steinfels, Margaret O. *Who's Minding the Children?* NewYork: Simon and Schuster, 1973.
Wolins, Martin and Irving Pliven. *Institution or Foster Family.* Washington, D.C.: Child Welfare League of America, 1964.

For juveniles and their courts
Chute, Charles Lionel and Marjorie Bell. *Crime, Courts and Probation.* New York: The Macmillan Co., 1956.
Rosenheim, Margaret Keeney. *Justice for the Child.* New York: The Free Press, 1962.
Killian, Frederick W. "The Juvenile Court as an Institution." *Annals of American Academy of Political and Social Science* CCLXI (January, 1949):89-101.
Rendelman, Douglas R. "*Parens Patriae*: From Chancery to the Juvenile Court." *South Carolina Law Review 23* (1971): 205-223.
National Probation Association. *The Yearbook of the National Probation Association.* New York: The National Probation Association, 1934/35/36.
Massachusetts House Report No. 2123, 1939.

Chapter Five

General histories of the New Deal:
Braeman, John Braeman, ed. *The New Deal.* Columbus: Ohio State University Press, 1975.

Burns, James MacGregor. *Roosevelt: The Lion and the Fox.* New York: Harcourt, Brace and World, Inc., 1956.
Trout, Charles H. *Boston, the Depression and the New Deal.* New York: Oxford University Press, 1977.

For children and the family:
Bremner, Robert, ed. *Children and Youth in America,* Vol. IV, parts 1 and 2. Cambridge: Harvard University Press, 1974.
Platt, Anthony M. *The Child Savers.* Chicago: University of Chicago Press, second edition, 1977.
Rosenheim, Margaret Keeney, ed. *Justice for the Child.* New York: The Free Press, 1962.
Schlossman, Steven L. *Love and the American Delinquent.* Chicago: University of Chicago Press, 1977.
Smith, Eva P. and Lisa A. Merkel-Holguin. *A History of Child Welfare.* New Brunswick: Transaction Publishers, 1969.
Steinfels, Margaret O'Brien. *Who's Minding the Children?* New York: Simon and Schuster, 1973.

Chapter Six

For the politics and social programs of the fifties, see Goldman, Eric F. *The Crucial Decade and After.* New York: Vintage Books, 1960.

Supreme Court decisions and commentary can be found in Alfred H. Kelly and Winfred A. Harbison. *The American Constitution,* 5th ed. New York: W.W. Norton and Company, 1976.

For Children's rights and Juvenile courts:

Bremner, Robert ed. *Children and Youth in America,* Vol. IV, part 2. Cambridge: Harvard U. Press. 1930-1974.
Hawes, James M. *The Children's Rights Movement.* Boston: Twayne Publishers, 1991.
Rosenheim, Margaret Keeney ed. *Justice for the Child.* New York: The Free Press, 1962.
Ryerson, Ellen. *The Best Laid Plans, America's Juvenile Court Experiment.* NewYork: Hill and Wang, 1978.
Steinfels, Margaret O'Brien. *Who's Minding the Children?* New York: Simon and Schuster, 1973.

Watkins, John C. Jr. *The Juvenile Justice Century.* Durham, NC: Caroline Academic Press, 1998.

Kurtz, Russell H., ed., *Social Work Yearbook.* New York: Russell Sage Foundation, 1947.

Handler, Joel F. "The Juvenile Court and the Adversary System: Problems of Function and Form." Vol. 1965 *University of Wisconsin Law Review*
(1965): 7-51.

Paulson, Monrad. "The Legal Framework for Child Protection." *Columbia Law Review.* 66 (1966): 682-687

Federal Probation. Vol. 49, no.2 *Juvenile Court and Family Journal.* (Fall, 1998).

Chapter Seven

Acerbic criticism of modern American social welfare policy can be found in Priven, Francis Fox and Richard A. Cloward. *Regulating the Poor.* New York: Vintage Books, 2nd ed., 1993.

Additional comments on social services in this era can be found in

Jenks, Christopher. *Rethinking Social Policy: Race, Poverty, and the Underclass.* Cambridge: Harvard University Press, 1992.

Smith, Eva P. Smith and Lisa A. Merkel-Holgin, eds. *A History of Child Welfare.* New Brunswick: Transaction Publishers, 1996.

Gilbert, Neil. "The Transformation of the Social Services." *Social Service Review* (December, 1977).

Zigler, Edward F., Sharon Lynn Kagan, Nancy W. Hall, eds. *Children, Families, and Government.* Cambridge University Press: New York, 1996.

Lemann, Nicholas. "The Unfinished War." *Atlantic Monthly* (December, 1988 and January, 1989).

Miller, Dorothy C. "AFDC: Mapping a Strategy for Tomorrow." *Social Service Review* (December, 1983).

Hunger in America was reviewed in the Physician Task Force on Hunger. *Hunger in America, the Growing Epidemic.* Middletown, Connecticut: Wesleyan University Press, 1985.

Observations about the truly disadvantaged come from

Levitan, Sar A. *Programs in Aid of the Poor.* Baltimore: The Johns Hopkins University Press, 1988.

Wilson, William Julius. *The Truly Disadvantaged.* Chicago: University of Chicago Press, 1987.

Observations about programs that work can be found in

Crane, Jonathan, ed. *Social Programs That Work.* New York: The Russell Sage Foundation, 1998.

Friedman, Lawrence M. "The Social and Political Context of the War on Poverty." Haverman, Robert H. ed. *A Decade of Anti-Poverty Programs.* New York: Harcourt, Brace, Janovich, 1977.

Discussion of income inequality comes from Danziger, Sheldon and Peter Gottschalk, eds. *Uneven Tides, Rising Inequality in America.* New York: Russell Sage Foundation, 1994.

Information about the debate, passage, effects of the President Clinton welfare bill was obtained by reading current journals like the *Economist* (September 30, 2000), but principally the *New York Times.* Articles authored by Jason de Parle. July 1994-December 1999.

Chapter Eight

Fahlberg, Vera I. *A Child's Journey Through Placement.* Indianapolis: Perspectives Press, 1991.

Goldstein, Joseph Albert J. Solnit, Anna Freud. *The Best Interests of the Child*, Revised. New York: The Free Press, 1996.

Hasci, Timothy A. *A Second Home, Orphan Asylums and Poor Families in America.* Cambridge: Harvard University Press, 1997.

Hawes, James M. *The Children's Rights Movement.* Boston: Twayne Publishers, 1991.

Platt, Anthony M. *The Child Savers.* Chicago: The University of Chicago Press, 1977.

Smith, Eve P. and Lisa A. Merkel-Holgun. *A History of Child_Welfare.* New Brunswick: Transaction Publishers, 1966.

Stein, Theodore J. *Child Welfare and the Law.* Washington, D.C.: Child Welfare League of America Press, 1998.

Waldfogel, Jane. *The Future of Child Protection.* Cambridge: Harvard University Press, 1998.

Foster, Henry Jr. and Doris Jonas Freed. "A Bill of Rights for Children. 6 *Family Law Quarterly*"(Winter 1972).

Mnookin, Robert. "Foster Care—In Whose Best Interest?" 43 *Harvard Educational Review*" Volume 4 (November 1973).

Weisman, Mary-Lou. "When Parents Are Not in the Best Interest of the Child," *Atlantic Monthly* (July, 1994).

The Children's Defense Fund. *The State of America's Children.* Boston: Beacon Press, 1998.

Child abuse reporting laws are covered in:

Campbell, Catherine E. "Neglected and Dependent Children," *Suffolk Law Review* Vol. IV, No.3 (Spring, 1970).
Page, Shippen "The Law, The Lawyer, and Medical Aspects of Child Abuse." In Eli Newberger, ed. *Child Abuse.* Boston: Little, Brown, 1982.
Discussion of the Chad Green case is in Arthur Harris Rosenberg. "Child Protective Legislation: Room for Improvement." *Boston Bar Journal* (September 1970).

Juvenile Law

A good review of juvenile court developments can be found in
Watkins, John C. *The Juvenile Justice Century.* Durham, North Carolina: Caroline Academics Press,1988.
National Council of Juvenile and Family Court Judges. *Juvenile and Family Court Journal,* Volume 49, Number 4, published by the National Council of Juvenile and Family Court Judges: Reno, Nevada (Fall 1998).
For the *Kent, Gault* and other case commentary:
Wadlington, Walter W., Charles H. Whitebread, and Samuel M. Davis. *Children in the Legal System.* Mineola, New York: The Foundation Press, 1983.
Clear, Michael G. "Problems of *In Re Gault,*" 2 *Suffolk Law Review* 1 (1968).
Melton, Gary B. "Taking *Gault* Seriously." 68 Nebraska Law Review. (1989).
Neigher, Alan. "The Gault Decision: Due Process and Juvenile Court." 31 *Federal Probation* (December 1967).
Phillips, Deborah. "Reconciling the Interests of Parent, Child and State." 15 *New England Law Review* (1979-1980).
Current data and analysis came from
Edelman, Marion Wright. *The State of America's Children.* Boston: Beacon Press, 1998.
The David and Lucille Packard Foundation. *The Future Of Children, the Juvenile Court.* Volume 6, Number 3, Winter,1996. Los Altos, CA:The David and Lucille Packard Foundation.
Citizens for Juvenile Justice. *Trends and Issues in Juvenile Delinquency.* Boston, 1999.
Information regarding the restoration of adult sentencing of juveniles was obtained from
Kotlowitz, Alex. "The Execution of Youth." *The New Yorker* (January 17, 2000).

Kauffmann, Sylvie. "Old Enough To Kill, Old Enough To Be Executed." December 2, 1999. Martin Kettle. "Judge Deals Blow to Penal Politics." January 20, 2000. Julian Borger. "US Kids Get Grown-Up Justice." March 23, 2000. In *Manchester Guardian Weekly*: Manchester, England.

Chapter Nine

Parental Rights

Stein,Theodore J. *Child Welfare and the Law.* Washington, D.C.: Child Welfare League of America Press, 1988.
The David and Lucille Packard Foundation. *The Future of Children, Protecting Children From Abuse and Neglect.* Vol. 8, No.1. Los Altos, CA: The David and Lucille Packard Foundation. (Spring 1998).

Family Courts

Flando, Carol R., Victor E. Flando and H. Ted Rubin. *How are Courts Coordinating Family Cases?* State Justice Institute, National Center for State Courts, 1999.
Hardin, Mark, H. Ted Rubin, Debra Ratterman Baker. *A Second Court That Works.* Clark Foundation, ABA, Center on Children and the Law, 1995.
Page, Robert W. *Family Courts: An Effective Judicial Approach to the Resolution of Family Disputes.* Juvenile and Family Court Journal, Vo.44, No.1, 1993, National Council of Juvenile and Family Court Judges, Reno, NV 1993.
Flynn, Colene. "Re-thinking *Lassiter*," 11 *Wisconsin Law Journal* (Fall 1996).

The David and Lucille Packard Foundation. *The Future of Children, The Juvenile Court,* Vol.6, No.3. Los Altos, CA: The David and Lucille Packard Foundation. (Winter 1996).
Massachusetts Bar Association. *The Massachusetts Courts in Crises: A Model for Reform* (June 1991).

Lassiter v. Department of Social Services, 452 U.S. 18,101 (1981).
Santosky v. Kramer, 102 Supreme Court, 1388 (1982).

Chapter Ten

Denise

York, John A., Leona B. Fredericks, John E. McManus, Barry L. Mintzer. *Report of the Child Abuse and Neglect Fact-Finding Commission.*

Studies and commentary, 1978-2000.
Massachusetts Acts and Resolves, 1978.
Court Files of Massachusetts Committee on Children and Youth.
Special Commission on Foster Care, Final Report, Volumes I and II, Published by Anderson Consulting, principle author Gael Mahoney, Esq., 1993.

Reports, opinions, analyses of poverty, policy and social service agencies as experienced by Massachusetts citizens
Boston Globe, September 15, 1991–April 4, 2000.

Personal Interviews, 1997–2000.

Massachussets

Jeanette Atkinson, Executive Director of Parents Helping Parents, Member of DSS Board that reviews deaths of children in DSS custody.

Charles D. Baker, Jr. Secretary of Health and Human Services during the early years of the creation of the modern DSS.

Joan Louden Black, DSS administrator.
Mary Byrne, Professor of Social Work, Boston College.
Jan Carey, Director, DSS multi-disciplinary team.
Corinne Contorino, Director of Boston's Patch project, Director of DSS Wareham Street Area Office.

Ted Cross, Brandeis University sociology statistician and researcher.
Walter Crowley, Ombudsman for DSS.
Eleanor Dowd, Reginal Director, DSS Region Four.
Maureen A. Ferris, Executive Director Massachusetts Children's Legislative Caucus.

Bridget Gassner, Attorney, Boston Juvenile Court.
Deborah Hobson, Director of CASA, Worcester, MA.
Trina Johnson, former probation officer, Boston Juvenile Court.
Sheila Kelley, Attorney, Boston Juvenile Court.
Amy Kremer, former DSS Attorney.
Mary Le Beau, Director, Mass Families for Kids.
Claire McCarthy, M.D., pediatrician at Martha Eliot neighborhood Health Center, author of *Everyone's Children*.

Mary McCree, private psychologist working with juvenile court judges in the Plymouth-Fall River area of Massachusetts.
John McManus, investigator in the case of Denise Galligan.
Maria Mosseides, Coordinator of Massachusetts Court Improvement Project.
Leah O'Leary, investigator in the case of Denise Galligan, DSS Area Program Manager, social work instructor.

Wanda Perry, DSS social worker.

Isabel Raskin, Attorney, Suffolk University Law School Juvenile Justice Center.

Arlene Rotman, Judge, Massachusetts Family and Probate Court.
Norma Sanchez, principal author of Kids Count, annual report on child abuse, issued by Massachusetts Committee on Children and Youth.

Catherine Sinnott, Attorney, Boston Juvenile Court.
Susan Stelk, Education coordinator, DSS.
Joy Tachuk, experienced foster mother in Salem, MA.
Ray Twomey, DSS attorney.
Elizabeth White, formerly DSS attorney, currently in private practice.
Patricia Woodley, DSS supervisor.

California:
William R. Gargano, Commissioner of Juvenile Court, San Francisco, CA
Michael Pearson, Research and Evaluation, Department of Social Services, Sacramento, CA.

Nancy Stone, Department of Social Services, Children's Services Operations Bureau, Sacramento, CA.

Connecticut:
Marylou Giovanucci, at the time of the interview, statewide coordinator of mediation services for the Department of Children and Families.

Michigan:
Ted Forrest, Manager, Child Protective Services, Lansing, MI.
Larry Leik, program analyst, Child Protective Services, Lansing, MI.

North Carolina:
Rebecca Brigham, Director of Social Work Training, North Carolina.
Daniel C. Hudgins, Director Durham County Department of Social Services.
Kennth C.Titus, Family Court Judge, Raleigh-Durham, NC.

Rhode Island:
Laureen D'Ambra, Director of the Office of Child Advocate, Providence, RI.
Jeremiah S. Jeremiah, Jr. Chief Judge Family Court, Providence, RI.

Wisconsin:
Attorney Richard Auerbach, children's advocate, Madison, WI.
Severa Austin, Division Administrator, Children, Youth and Families, Madison, WI.

Susan Crowley, Director, Children, Youth and Families, Madison, WI.
Ami E. Orlin, Project Director, Safe Harbor, Madison, WI.

Author's Biography

Attorney Susan G. Neisuler followed a career of teaching history with a career practicing law. She worked in the Boston Juvenile Court, where she encountered daily the problems of juveniles and families who had stumbled into the unwelcome arms of the social welfare/juvenile justice system. She resigned from her practice in order to research and write about the history of children under government control and the agencies that serve them and their families.

0-595-26950-8